Spirits of the Earth

Jaq D Hawkins

Illustrated by Jeremy Scott

Spirits of the Earth

Cover design by Paul Mason

Published by:

Capall Bann Publishing
Freshfields
Chieveley
Berks
RG20 8TF

Acknowledgements

Thanks go out to Kevin Bullimore for predicting that I should write this series of books, to my husband Jeremy for patiently (well, maybe not so patiently) allowing me to get on with it as well as for offering some valuable tidbits of information and reference materials, and to all of the Earthy people who have contributed to my understanding of the importance of this element and all that it represents in my own life and in the nature of magic and natural law itself.

Dedicated to my own fairy child,
Wendy LeFay

The Author

Jaq D. Hawkins began magical study as a child and has been aware of elemental spirits from a very young age, despite a primarily urban upbringing. Her writings on various aspects of magical law are recognized in American as well as British occult magazines and are repeated on various computer networks. Her writings on the relationship of elemental spirits to these natural laws is unique to this series of books. Ms. Hawkins currently lives in the North of England with her family.

The Illustrator

Jeremy Scott is a native of North Yorkshire where he attended Harrogate College of Arts. He has sold his artwork in private galleries as well as doing commissioned work, primarily his astoundingly realistic technical drawings. More recently, he has also become known for his striking land-scapes. He has diversified his talents into designing theatre sets, illustrating children's books and has even tried his hand at specialised interior design in San Francisco. His special talent for incorporating elemental creatures into his drawings is a valuable asset to this series.

Also by the Author:
    Understanding Chaos Magic

Books in Progress;
    Spirits of the Air
    Spirits of the Fire
    Spirits of the Water

Contents

Introduction to the Spirits of the Elements Series

The Spirits of the Elements series began when a friend of mine who is a palmist told me in a reading that I was destined to write a series of books about nature spirits. At first, I tried to associate this prediction with a series of children's books which I was working on at the time, as it involves characters and events taken directly from my studies about elemental spirits. However, my friend insisted that this was not the series of which he spoke. There would be a series of books written for an adult audience which he was looking forward to reading.

At first, I wondered if the material would have been sufficiently covered by books already in print, However, this concern melted away as the chapters began to form in my mind.

I believe in fairies. Call them what you will, I believe that the spirits of natural, and some things which would seem at first as not natural, exist whether or not we choose to believe in them. These elemental spirits are very much a part of our world which we cannot afford to ignore or dismiss if we are to understand our own magical nature, or that which draws us into the world of magic.

The four alchemical elements are Earth, Air, Fire and Water References to these four elements are used in many forms of Paganism and Magic. They represent the material world for

Earth, inspiration for Air, determination for Fire, and emotion for Water. There is a fifth element called Aether. This represents spirit.

In the following chapters, I will explain the associations and correspondences which humans have attached to the element for this volume, but let's not forget that this is essentially a book about nature spirits. It is their nature that I hope to express in these pages. I also hope to offer some practical information about the methods of perceiving these spirits and perhaps inviting them into the home or into ritual practices. One must remember that these entities cannot be commanded, only invited. I strongly recommend respecting their independence. It is no accident that old tales about fairies often warn of danger, or at least trickery! More about that later.

One quick note for those who wish to see fairies; visual perception is rare but not unknown. They are not physically perceived with the eye in the same way as solid objects. If one studies the medical information learned over many years about how the eye perceives line and colour, one learns that there are receptors in the eyeball called rods and cones. The rods, which are shaped as the name would suggest, perceive line and definition while the cones, which are shaped like little round cones (what a surprise) perceive colour. The combined messages are sent to the brain and we 'see' things as a whole comprising defined shape and colour.

Seeing nature spirits requires a shift in our perception because the rods in our eyes perceive nothing from them. It is the cones which can perceive nature spirits, which is why they are so often depicted as brightly coloured and fanciful little creatures. To an extent, their shape is defined by what we expect it to be. It is also because they are perceived with the cones that they become elusive when one tries to look directly at them. Cones perceive periphially. To see a fairy, one must try to catch it with the corner of one's eye. Perhaps this is at least part of the reason that so many people find it difficult to believe that they were ever there at all...

1

The Nature of Earth

Earth is nature itself in its most obvious form to the human observer. The terra firma on which we stand and spend our lives is as essential to our survival as the air we breath. Perhaps even more so as we would have no air without the Earth on which plants and trees grow, creating oxygen to breath.

Most of the nature spirits that come to mind when we think of fairies are Earth spirits. Fairies of flowers, rocks, plants, trees and many other associations are Earth spirits. When we play charades and ask if something is animal, mineral or vegetable, we are referring to things which are all associated with Earth.

Earth is the building block of all that is in the material world, which is why Earth, as an alchemical element, represents the material existence of all things. Earth, in magic, represents the material world and things associated with it such as health, prosperity and mundane concerns.

However, that does not make it any less spiritual as an element than any of the others; Air, Fire, Water and Aether. The pentacle which represents the Earth element in many well known magical systems also represents the foundations of the magic itself. In ceremonial magick, it represents (among other things) the magician's body which is considered to be a temple and according to the beliefs of some, it is where the construction of the magic takes place. Some subscribers to these beliefs are more specific and feel that the magical energy emanates specifically from the mind of the magician, but this also must have the solid foundation of the brain which in turn is part of the physical body.

Without Earth, we have nothing on which to construct. Without our bodies, we have nothing in which to personalise our soul. Some would say that that would be an advantage, and I'm sure that there is plenty of scope for after-death or astral magic, but as long as we are contained within our bodies, we shall continue to have an Earth temple within which we may perform magic to affect our very Earthly environment. If we are honest with ourselves, much of the magic that is done by modern witches and magicians is very much directed at affecting something on the Earth plane.

Eco-magicians are very attuned to the Earth element. Saving our Earthly environment may well require an understanding of the symbolic relationships among all of the elements, but the focus is undeniably directed on the Earth element. Whether a Pagan or Magician worships among the trees in a forest, builds a temple of stone or performs magic solely within the confines of his or her own physical body, the basis for all magic is firmly set in some form of an Earth based physical structure. In some cases, this may be the planet itself.

This could all begin to sound rather claustrophobic. Wherever you go, whatever you do, the Earth and the needs of the material existence surround you. There is no escape.

And therein lies the understanding of the magic of the Earth element. Without a solid basis, there can be no magic. The mundane world that many strive to rise above is an integral part of the lofty ideals of spirituality which some may try to ignore, but can never really overcome. In nature, there is no quest to overcome the material world. The material world is very much a part of nature, and the natural reaction to any living thing to a need within the material world is to seek satisfaction of the need within the natural rhythms of nature.

A hungry animal will seek food, a thirsty plant will reach through the Earth with its roots to seek water. Religions which strive to become pure spirit are attempting to deny the solid basis of flesh and Earthly needs. This is unnatural not only for humans and other animals, but also in the balance of the universe as we know it. There is balance in nature. It is only humankind's arrogance which strives to deny the basis of the natural world.

In magic, the Earth element is commonly invoked for purposes associated with the material, or the planet itself. These include healing spells, prosperity spells, planet healings and any number of purposes that involve the physical world. Many magical systems invoke some aspect of divinity which rules over these Earthly purposes during these spells, some even invoke the nature spirits themselves. How much these spirits comply with such invocations is another matter, one is far more likely to create thoughtform elementals in response to a nature spirit invocation than to actually attract a spirit out of its natural habitat.

To actually experience a nature spirit, one must visit the natural habitat of that spirit. Those of us who truly believe in these spirits believe that every tree, every stone (particularly standing stones) and all things in nature are inhabited and looked after by resident spirits. Several books have been written about the Findhorn community in Scotland where people often report communing with nature spirits.

Other books have been written about fairy kingdoms and individuals who have experienced Earth spirits in some manner. *The Real World of Fairies*, by Dora Van Gelder is an excellent example. There are more, many of which are listed in the Bibliography of this volume. There is still dispute about the authenticity of the Cottingley Fairies, but one must wonder when reports of fairy sightings have continued throughout written history in some form, quite often with similar characteristics.

The consensus is that the growing things of the Earth are cared for by nature spirits commonly referred to as fairies, which are not normally visible to the human eye. However, these are not the only 'fairies' which are commonly reported. There are many legends of tricky or even severely nasty forms of fairies which do mischief to humans. Many of these are reported as rather less attractive to the eye than the pretty little images of flower fairies and such like.

By now the reader may be fuming over the fact that I have not mentioned house fairies. Many of these are Earth spirits as well, and will not be neglected here. Kitchen fairies are generally associated with the Earth element, as are many spirits which inhabit household objects of various kinds. We must keep in mind however, that associations of spirits with specific elements is largely a matter of human perceptions and categorisation, I will write about house fairies in more detail in a later chapter, as most of them fall into the category of thought-form elementals.

Still, all of the spirits I have mentioned are Earth spirits for the purposes of this book. With very few exceptions, most of the legendary bogies and brownies, hobgoblins and the like are all associated with Earth. Many a traveller has been afraid to enter a remote forest for fear of the spirits that may seek to protect their habitat from the ravages of humankind. These are spirits which are very close to the Earth and whatever aspect of the Earth element that is in its keeping, whether it is a living plant or tree, or simply a rock in the forest.

Spirits of standing stones are particularly strong and easy for the sensitive person to perceive (if not actually see) because their habitat is something which is used to amplify the magical currents of the Earth itself. Stories have been told of religious fanatics attempting to bring down stone circles, only to have one of these massive stones fall onto and crush one of their party, usually the leader of the group. Reports from people who have visited Stonehenge after dark often mention an uneasy feeling there at night. The spirits of the stones know how to protect themselves.

However, standing stone spirits can be powerful allies if given proper respect. I am fortunate enough to live near a small grouping of dolmen stones which are well known in the area, yet not one of the major tourist attractions. The spirits of these stones are familiar friends to me. I visit them occasionally, quite often in connection with spells, but sometimes simply to 'commune' with them. I make a point of sharing energy with them rather than always asking for extra charges for my spells, and of affording them the respect that might be considered appropriate for an icon, yet not to the extent of deifying them.

Earlier I spoke of Earth as the solidity on which all magic is based, but there is another side to the Earth element which must be recognized. Earth spirits are not all cutsie flower fairies prancing in the forest, or mischievous goblins drying up the local milk cow. The Earth has a way of cleansing and renewing itself which can be very frightening to a mere human who gets in the way of natural phenomena. As a wise man I know has often said, "Nature eats its own".

The power of the Earth, particularly amplified in some way, is a tremendous force to reckon with. It is displayed in natural form in such things as earthquakes and volcanos, demonstrating the power of the primordial chaos of destruction and creation. We may view these events as catastrophes when human life is lost through them, yet for the Earth itself the creative principle is just as well represented in the results of the event. New land formations are created during these 'disasters', and inner energies of the Earth released for some purpose that has little or nothing to do with the human dwellings and lives which may be swept away should they fall into the path of one of these Earthly power surges.

Some forces are simply beyond human limitations to harness or control, and the best we can do is to try to get out of the way. Primitive human societies who have come into regular contact with these Earth forces have believed in spirits such as those who bring earthquakes or ruling spirits of volcanos. What many people don't realise is that these beliefs are still rather widespread, although appeasing an angry volcano spirit seldom results in throwing in a virgin sacrifice anymore.

Temples, churches and standing stones are humankind's way of trying to focus a manageable amount of this natural energy, success depending on the level of understanding that is put into the construction and use of these manmade amplifiers. There have been many studies and speculations about ancient temples which appear to have been made by someone with an understanding of shapes and constructions, even locations, which are conducive to amplification of Earth energies. Pyramids are one example, and there are many more.

The stone circles in Britain and some parts of Continental Europe have given rise to much speculation as to their original purposes. While the observatory theory may be the most widely accepted, there is quite a lot of evidence which suggests that these stone monuments actually serve to amplify the Earth's natural electromagnetic energies. Carefully shaped Earth mounds, such as Glastonbury Tor in Southwest England and the Great Serpent Mound in Ohio, USA are also connected to speculations about amplified Earth energies, associations with Earth spirits, and any number of stories and legends which suggest that there is more to them than a bit of creative sculpting.

The Earth itself has long been deified as the Mother Goddess by some religions, particularly pre-Christian religions in agricultural communities. The Earth gives forth life, because it gives forth food to the farmers, and is therefore the nurturing queen of the food chain which allows humans and other animals to thrive upon her.

Her helpers, the 'wee folk' who care for the growing things and have become known to us as "fairies", "devas" and many other names, are the best known spirits of the Earth. Our fascination with these spirits, whether we believe that they are no more than old superstitions and "fairy tales" or whether we believe that they are actual beings who inhabit the planet keeping themselves well away from humans, is a subject which holds the imaginations of many people today.

Some legends of fairies may well come from situations where there is a logical explanation. There is anthropological evidence which suggests that a small, dark race of people may have existed on the high dune known as Skara Brae on the Orkney mainland in the north of Scotland several centuries ago. These people would have been invaded and pushed into hiding by the Vikings who settled in the area. The need to survive could easily drive such a race of people to scavenge food in whatever way they could, including stealing supplies from the settlers. One can imagine that if a small dark person were seen in the vicinity of the barn in the early hours when the family cow had been dry for some time, one might jump to the conclusion that this 'fairy person' had cast a spell against the family. The more logical explanation, that the small person had been creeping in early to milk the cow for his own family, might not be as obvious to a superstitious society.

However, these potential explanations are few and far between. There are many more legends of fairies and other nature spirits which defy explanation. The purpose of this book is not to make a case for the existence of Earth spirits, but to speak of their nature, assuming existence. Those who do not believe will probably never read these pages.

As we attach attributes of the alchemical elements to nature spirits, we can remember that it is easy to do so because the spirits themselves attach themselves to things in nature. The spirit of a lake is obviously a Water spirit, the spirit of a windstorm is obviously an Air spirit. Earth spirits are spirits which are attached to things of the Earth, or material things in any form.

As humans, we create correspondences between things and create models of 'systems' which help us to better understand the natural world and things like the laws of physics which can be complicated, even with a great deal of education. The Earth moves and changes in ways that some people understand better than others, yet in learning to understand the nature of spirit, we may find that we understand those things which the scientists are still unable to measure, weigh and categorise.

In understanding the spirits which we associate with the things of Earth and the solid foundations of natural magic, we bring ourselves closer to an understanding of the balance in the universe and the aspect of that balance which we signify by the solid building blocks, and the very creative principle, which we call Earth.

2

Types of Earth Spirits

Earth spirits abound in legends and stories from every culture. Western culture has historically attached a great deal of superstition to "the wee folk", while many other cultures simply accept them as part of the natural world. It is only since Victorian times that fairies' have been perceived as fanciful creatures who resemble pretty little girls (and sometimes boys) with butterfly wings, and only in the past few decades that much of the superstition inherent in our culture has given way to an understanding of the balance in nature that we share with plants, animals, and many things which are unseen. To those who believe in magic and nature religions, this balance is illustrated by the four alchemical elements; Earth, Air, Fire and Water. For some, this must also include a fifth element, the element of Spirit called Aether.

Many of the most widely known forms of Elemental Spirits; fairies, bogies, etc., are associated with Earth. Personalities have been attributed to these traditional spirits by (usually) country peoples who have believed in them for centuries and felt that they were a part of life with which they must reckon in their daily routines. A few samples of some of those which have been written about by 'experts' are as follows, keep in mind that these examples are at least partly perceived through superstition:

SPRIGGANS (British)

Spriggans are reputed to be rather nasty and unattractive spirits, possibly the ghosts of old giants, who are known for thieving and for stealing babies, leaving a changling of their own in exchange. They can be bargained with or even repulsed by Holy Water or by turning one's clothing inside out. They are capable of robbing human houses, blighting crops, bringing whirlwinds and other destructive acts.

GHILLIE DHU (Scottish)

A solitary fairy who inhabits birch thickets in Scotland. His clothing is made from leaves and moss.

LEPRECAUN (Irish)

Most people have heard of these. They are specifically Irish, and particularly known for hiding pots of gold. One children's legend tells us that we can find the pot of gold at the end of the rainbow, but an older version of this requires that one catch the Leprecaun, in order to force the Leprecaun to turn over his gold in exchange for his freedom. Some tales also claim that the Leprecaun must grant three wishes to the lucky human by whom he was caught. Oddly, there seldom seem to be female Leprecauns. A less widely known aspect of the Leprecaun is the change which comes over him at night, when he becomes the **CLURICAUN** and raids cellars as well as riding drunkenly on the backs of sheep.

FIR DARRIG (Irish)

One of the practical joking nature spirits. It is considered wise to humour him.

GOBLIN or BOGIE

A general term used for ugly fairies, but also a specific term used for small, malicious beings. Some of these are shapeshifters and will appear as animals. They are a tricky breed who will lure human victims to their own destruction.

KOBOLDS, WICHTLEIN (German), COBLYNAU (Welsh) and KNOCKERS (Cornish)

These are names for mining spirits. Kobolds and Knockers are trouble makers who will undo the day's work for the human miners. The Wichlein are harbingers of impending doom. They will announce the impending death of a miner by tapping three times. The Coblynau, on the other hand, are harmless spirits who simply imitate the human miners and are actually considered to be good luck.

DWARFS (Saxon)

Dwarfs are considered to be short, muscular and bearded. They are another mining spirit, but are also reputed to work in metals and to fashion very fine weapons and jewellery. Some legends say that they cannot come into the daylight, or that they turn into toads during the daytime.

PIXIES (Cornish)

These have become a popular focus of the tourist trade in Devon and Cornwall. Pixies are sometimes called Urchins. They take the form of hedgehogs and can be either mischievous or agreeable. Some may steal horses or take wild night rides on the wild Dartmoor ponies, while others may work hard threshing corn at night for rewards of bread and cheese.

PHOOKA (Irish)
The Phooka is a shape-shifter which may take the form of a dog, horse, bull or even a goat or eagle. He offers a lift to the unwary traveller, then takes him on a wild ride across rough country before dumping him unceremoniously in a ditch or mire. The Phooka enjoys a good laugh this way.

TROLL (Scandinavian)
Trolls are generally unattractive, bad-tempered, muscular beings who cause mischief. They dislike daylight, and sometimes live under bridges in order to catch travellers to eat for their dinner.

BROWNIE (British)
These go by regional names; Bwca in Wales, Bodach in the Highlands of Scotland and Fenoderee on the Isle of Man. They are house spirits which come out at night and perform various chores. They are often left gifts of cream and cake spread with honey by the humans who inhabit their adopted homes. It is considered wise to stay in favour with the house Brownie, as they can easily change character and become a troublesome Boggart.

This is only a small sampling of the types of Earth spirits which humans have traditionally believed in over the centuries and is by no means a comprehensive list. It would require a large volume to make a dictionary of such spirits, and would require many examples from all cultures which inhabit our planet. Names for spirits of similar types vary from one country to another, and as shown in some of the above examples, can also vary regionally.

Perhaps the most famous race of Earth spirits in our culture is the Tuatha de Danaan, an Irish race of fairies who are the subjects of legends of valour which have shaped the tales of fairy kindred for hundreds of years and influenced relatively modern fantasy writers like J.R.R. Tolkien.

Traditional fairies are only one type of Earth spirit, but in fact they hold as much reality to those who believe in them and encounter them as the less fanciful elemental spirits which inhabit the natural world. Fancy can lead to reality, as will be more fully explained in a later chapter. There is more than imagination to credit for the reported encounters with traditional fairies and goblins, as well as sightings of what one may call 'pretty fairies'.

Victorian art holds a wealth of fanciful representations of fairies and spirits. The still-famous Cottingley Fairies and the Flower Fairies drawn by Cicely Mary Barker are good examples of the fanciful notions of these Earth spirits which have become a popular vision of fairies.

It can be easy to forget while enjoying these pretty bits of artwork that all of the old legends about elemental spirits repeatedly warn against trespassing on fairy ground or offending the 'wee folk' in any way, yet we are occasionally reminded of this by old legends which warn of trespassing in certain places, or even by modern films which are more frequently attempting to portray fairies in a manner based on modern perceptions. For example, in the film *Labyrinth*, which stars David Bowie as the Goblin King, the heroine's first encounter with pretty little girl fairies results in a nasty bite. This is followed by a variety of encounters with assorted muppet goblins who play all sorts of tricks on her, not unlike what one would expect of the legendary antics of Brownies and Boggarts, given the same situation.

That isn't to say that Earth spirits are necessarily mischievous or nasty by nature, they simply have their own social rules, and ignorance of their values can have disastrous results for the unwary trespasser. Elemental spirits are very close to nature, and all too often we humans take it all for granted and one might say we deserve what we get in return.

A more modern perception of Earth spirits has come to us through writings about a garden inhabited by these spirits in a caravan park in Scotland, called Findhorn. Several books have been written about life at Findhorn by visitors and residents of the caravan park. These books tell us about spirits (referred to as devas) who care for the garden, and about a style of living which involves feeling close to these spirits while caring for the garden and eating the vegetables which are made all the more nourishing by the care with which the devas have lavished on them. Every cabbage or plant of any kind has its own deva to care for it. The natural world is filled with spirits for every plant, tree or even rock. They are the caretakers of the things in nature. In Findhorn, the existence of these helpful garden spirits is evidenced by amazing results in the garden, which is grown under seemingly adverse conditions. The ability of the residents of Findhorn to grow unusually large vegetables in rocky, sandy soil with cold, Highland winds blowing fiercely across the surface is remarkable to say the least.

This view of guardian nature spirits has caught on extremely well in just a couple of decades, and has shaped the perceptions of elemental spirits in our culture to an incredible degree. The reason for this may be that we have only just begun, through the channellings which occur in Findhorn, to accurately perceive these spirits. The view of nature spirits as guardians of the things in nature is actually a very old concept, one which has been known in Eastern and Aboriginal cultures for centuries.

Interestingly, R. Olgilvie Crombie (who is associated with the Findhorn Community) reports encounters with nature spirits whom he has perceived in the form of fauns and the god Pan himself, which come from Greek legends. The images which we hold of nature spirits and how they should appear are largely a personal perception. They seem to appear in a variety of ways to different people who are able to perceive them, yet the nature of the spirits and their purpose in the natural world is something which we are beginning to understand universally, regardless of our individual perceptions of their appearance and individual characteristics.

American Indians are traditionally attuned to spirits in nature, as are most aboriginal cultures. In films we are made aware of the Indian perception of animal spirits, yet Hollywood has largely ignored the application of this belief to plant and tree spirits. Occasionally, the spirit of a place, particularly a rocky outcrop, will make it into the script. In the real world, aboriginal peoples from any part of the world are likely to believe in guardian spirits of places as well as animals or indigenous vegetation. Sickness is attributed to evil spirits or to angry spirits, offended by something the sick person has done. Cures are effected by appeasing the offended spirit or by driving out the spirit, often with astonishing success.

The Polynesian peoples are another good example of this. Keeping the local spirits happy is a very old and traditional part of everyday life in island cultures, particularly in places prone to earthquakes and volcano eruptions. A volcano god is every bit as much an Earth Spirit as the pretty little fairies in your garden.

The concept of powerful spirits and 'lower' spirits exists in many forms. Dora Van Gelder writes of an actual hierarchy of nature spirits, which to an extent appears to be echoed by the Findhorn perception of the spirit world. The idea of an actual hierarchy as we think of such a system is too militaristic to accurately describe what is in actuality a symbiotic system within the natural world where concepts of rank and rulership have no real place. Too often, our human minds must classify things in a manner which we can understand and the true nature of something which is very different to the things we have been taught all of our lives can be difficult to comprehend. Using terms which can be misconstrued leads to mistaken notions which are passed from one person to another rather like 'Chinese whispers' and results in a total misconception of that which we are trying to understand.

A spirit of a common stone is not lower than a garden pixie or a ruling spirit of a magical site, it is simply different in nature. Just as Air spirits differ from Fire spirits, different types of spirits within the classification of 'Earth spirits' occur in a vast array of forms, These forms may include some fanciful as well as house spirits, but the vast majority of what we mean by the term "Earth spirits" or elementals are the spirits of objects in nature.

3

Abodes of Earth Spirits

One way of identifying nature spirits is through their associations with natural habitats. The tenets of many nature religions include a belief that every tree, rock, flower or object of any sort comes with an attendant spirit to watch over and nurture it, as was described earlier in the case of the Findhorn community. However, this concept is not new. It is simply becoming more widely known due to the amount of literature which has been appearing on the subject in the past few decades.

One of my favourite artists, Jeremy Scott (who graciously consented to illustrate this series), frequently includes subtle nature spirits in his drawings. One must look closely at his drawings to notice the delicate grass fairies and rock spirits which appear in the backgrounds, and sometimes in the foregrounds, of his drawings and paintings.

These depictions come from an understanding of the diversity of nature spirits and their habitats which happens on an intuitive level among those who believe in elemental spirits and seek to be close to them in some way or another.

In a way, the human concept of hierarchy among nature spirits is simply an association with the size of an individual spirit's domain. Small spirits, such as the spirit of a single blade of grass, are often thought of as insignificant to the human mind, yet these little fairies are essential beings in the elemental world every bit as much as a mighty oak spirit. Examples of small spirits are the spirits of grass, flowers and small stones. Stone spirits are easier to 'sense' if the stone contains some quartz, as quartz crystals conduct electromagnetic energy which is more perceptible to humans than other minerals which may lack this extra electrical charge, but the spirits of the stones are just as 'alive' whether we are able to perceive them or not.

Gemstone spirits, whether the stones are unmined or set into a piece of jewellery, are rather powerful little spirits which magicians have used for magical purposes for centuries. Outside of the natural world, there are small spirits in many objects in the ordinary human world. The herbs in your kitchen cupboard may well still be looked after by the spirits who once helped them grow.

Certain mechanical things, such as clocks, may also have attendant spirits which have come into being through the purpose of the object. As is explained elsewhere in this book, a spirit can be created for an inanimate object through human attention, although these spirits are different from spirits which occur in nature.

One of the most familiar forms of Earth spirits which inhabit human inventions is commonly known as a "computer gremlin". These are the spirits which create chaos for computer users by making the machine behave in ways that cannot be explained through a knowledge of technology. While often treated as a joke by the well-educated computer progr- ammer, these spirits are very real and can be reasoned with if one uses the correct approach.

Spirits of larger flowers and medium sized plants are most likely to resemble our common conceptions of fairies. These can occur in the wild as well as in a cultivated garden, but it is up to us to remember that our images of them come largely from our own imaginations as the colour wavelengths in which spirit forms are perceived are very much at the edge of the capability of the human eye to perceive and the brain will fill in details very much in the same way that it fills in the 'black spot' in the centre of our visual field.

Spirits of larger rocks are similar in nature to those of pebbles and smaller rocks, but are likely to be perceived as larger to accommodate the added size of their natural habitat. It is not unusual to 'sense' the presence of these sorts of spirits in various places, although many people fail to realise that it is the spirits they are sensing when they refer to the "feeling" of a place. For those who wish to become aware of the spirit world, it is worth noting the sorts of objects which occur in the places we visit whether it is our own back garden or an out-of-the-way place we are visiting, and to imagine what sort of spirits may attend the place and the things which we see.

It seems that the larger the object, the more vibrant the attending spirit is likely to be. A tree spirit, particularly the spirit of a very large and old tree, can feel rather imposing where the spirit of a medium sized bush is likely to seem more personal and friendly. It is easy to imagine very large standing stones and old oak trees assuming the bearing of gods to the early Druids, or to imagine the effect of a powerful volcano spirit on primitive peoples.

The attending spirits of these larger natural objects may be every bit as friendly as the smaller garden fairies, yet they inspire awe and respect by their very presence. Some of the reason for this lies with our own perceptions of bigger = more powerful, yet there is also a primal understanding within us of the natural hierarchy in nature as well as the instinctive realisation that there are forces more powerful than ourselves, regardless of whatever ideas we may hold about humankind's mastery over the natural world. On the bottom line, we know within ourselves that nature could wipe us off the face of the planet with a gravitational shift if we interfere too much.

One might ask, just where do these nature spirits live, or exist? Understanding this is made difficult by our knowledge of solid objects and three-dimensional space. If we see ourselves living in constructed homes and think of nature as little animals living in burrows, tree trunks and other enclosures, then it is only natural to think of nature spirits as having some form of homes to return to at the end of the day. This has been dealt with in art and cartoons by depicting fairies sleeping in the blossoms of flowers, among the leaves in a cabbage, or any number of similar places. Trolls, gnomes and other Earth spirits are said in stories to sleep under bridges, in mountain villages or underground.

What we must remember is that we are talking about the realm of spirit. Just as our 'souls' inhabit our bodies, the nature spirits inhabit an object or a particular space. There is a difference in that nature spirits can commonly be found in the area surrounding their object or space, very much as if they were an external being, while a very small percentage of humans have learned to "astral project" themselves outside of their immediate bodies and fewer still have any concept as to why this art should be learned.

This is an area where we can very definitely learn valuable lessons from nature. A magician may learn to astral project, and perhaps even explore the uses that such a state can be put to, yet it is not very common for these same magicians to ask themselves why this ability is possible. All things in nature have a purpose. Given that nature spirits project beyond their immediate abodes in order to "attend" them, I will leave it to the reader to imagine in what manner a human spirit might model the workings of nature.

Thinking of Earth spirits as the attendant spirits of various places and objects can explain much of the superstition and legend which we have passed down through stories over the centuries, but what about the legendary 'Land of Faery'? Some of the stories about spirits who live within magical hillsides or mountains could be explained away through careful analysis of old stories, but this sort of rational dissection and classification of facts means very little to those who have, at some time in their lives, actually wandered into an experience with the 'other' world.

Many similar stories have been told about experiences with hill fairies in particular. An example is related in *Images and Oracles of Austin Osman Spare* by Kenneth Grant. The young magician was walking through a snowstorm out in the country where he had been visiting friends, and was beginning to be overcome with cold and exhaustion when a pony-trap appeared. He was helped on board and after what seemed like a long journey, was deposited at the gates of an inn. A man in old-fashioned clothing beckoned him inside and gave him some of the best wine he had ever tasted, then described the best way to return to his friend's home.

Later, he described his experience to his friends who insisted that no such place existed. Spare remembered the way to the inn, and as it had stopped snowing just before he had entered it, there were plenty of footsteps to follow. When they all returned the next day, the footsteps led to a mound which was all that remained of an inn which had existed 300 years earlier. This is not the only 'otherworld' experience that Spare experienced in his life. Similar experiences by other people have led them to follow their own tracks to hillsides where they abruptly stopped, usually after an evening of enjoying food and drink with strange folk in the remembered place. While some of these stories may well be the stuff of folktales, my own experience with a place which leads to an important experience and then effectively disappears, only to be replaced by something completely different, is enough to convince me that not all of the stories are folktales, exaggerations, or the result of drinking too much.

In my experience, I was 14 years old. I had never tried drugs and very seldom tasted alcohol at that time. I was walking in an area which was in the process of being built up to become a suburb of a larger city, but still had a lot of open fields. At one point, I was about a mile from home and was getting tired of walking, so instead of doubling the distance by following the roads, I decided to cross the open fields.

I could actually see where I wanted to be in the distance. Somehow I knew or could see from the land configurations that I would have to cross three separate fields which I would soon learn were divided by a road and then a small stream. I remember that the three sections just looked different from where I stood.

The first field was a simple field of knee-high grass. There was a slight rise which kept me from clearly seeing the second field until I was very close to it, but I crossed it quickly and came to the road. On the opposite side of the road was a low wire fence, and then a very odd thing happened. I was confronted not by another field, but by a forest of dead trees. They were unlike any trees I have seen before or since. I had no way to identify them. They were about five feet tall, completely bare, and very ominous looking.

The decision to climb the fence and continue was not an easy one. There was more to see among the dead trees than I will relate here as it involves an encounter with Air spirits rather than Earth spirits, but I was very much aware that I had stumbled into an 'otherworld'. In the end, I decided to continue, knowing within myself that I would be safe so long as I didn't feel fear. I passed through this place, eventually coming to the stream. I began to cross, and then began to sink. It could have been a very awkward situation as I was soon sinking as far as my knees with each step, but I stayed calm and pressed forward, lifting my feet out of the all-consuming sand with more difficulty with each step. The ground actually got more solid in the middle where there seemed to be some sort of sand island, then wasn't very difficult after that.

The opposite bank was sandy but dry, and I finished my journey home without further incident. I decided on the way that I would have to retrace my steps with camera in hand in the near future. It was only a couple of months before I did. Rather than returning to this place directly from home, I decided that I wanted to retrace my steps as they had happened the first time. So, I followed the roads to my previous starting point. The first thing that struck me was that it wasn't quite as easy to see my destination from the distance. It was definitely the same place, yet it somehow seemed farther away.

The first field was very much as it had been on the first journey. The grass was just a bit longer, but there was the same rise and the same road with the same fence. That was where the sameness stopped. On the other side of the fence was a very different place with lush grass and tall trees of a rather tropical sort. The feeling that had accompanied the dead tree forest was non-existent. I climbed the fence without hesitation and tried to follow my previous path. Eventually I happened across a workman on a tractor who gave me a ride across what he explained was a duck sanctuary, showing me the lake on the way. The place had been there for years, it was owned by the local college.

I had managed to follow my original course rather closely as I could tell when I came to the stream. My footprints were still there on the sand island. I hesitated about crossing because of my previous sinking experience, but being too young and lazy to go back, I tried a tentative step to see what would happen. This time, the sand under the water was quite solid and I didn't sink more than an inch at any point as I crossed. Again, I reached the sandy bank and followed my previous course without further incident.....and without having taken any photographs.

The nature of the 'otherworld' of Faery is not easily explained, even by those who have experienced it. To relate this sort of experience to the concept of nature spirits as the guardians of plants, rocks, etc. requires that one remembers again that this is a world of spirit which we are talking about and that these nature spirits always live within the 'otherworld' which a few of us may stumble into on occasion.

Just a few moments of experiencing this 'otherworld' is generally enough to make anyone appreciate the need to work in harmony with Earth spirits when attending a garden or doing anything which affects nature. It is a far more satisfying feeling than any attempt to gain mastery over the things of the natural world.

In general though, the spirit world relates closely to our material world in a geographical sense. Places seen in the 'otherworld' will coincide to our world, with perhaps a change in one specific land formation. There is always something like a "fairy mound" to replace a remembered inn, or the 'otherworld' place will fit neatly into the geography of another place which exists in the material world such as in my own experience.

This may help to explain why certain places in our ordinary world become associated with fairies or spirits of some kind, and why sightings of these spirits are more frequently reported in these places. It would seem that specific places are conducive to crossing the lines that divide the spirit and material worlds.

4

Places to Find Earth Spirits

Deep inside the fairy glade
There lies a realm where Magic' s made
Where fair few mortal head has laid
yet ever once a champion is bade...

...Anonymous

Magical places abound throughout the world. Some are well known and attract visitors by the hundreds, while others remain relatively unknown and attract only the occasional passer-by. The fact that people are attracted to these places at all is a matter of the 'spirit of the place'.

Psychically sensitive people can sense the spirit of any place, but magical place spirits vibrate so strongly that even those with very little sensitivity can be overwhelmed by the feeling of 'spirit' in certain places. The exact nature of 'place spirits' is the subject of this chapter.

How one defines 'spirit' can get in the way of understanding the nature of this form of spirit. Some may perceive a place spirit as a personified spirit in and of itself, but in fact the

spirit of a place is most often a conglomeration of the combined spiritual elementals which care for and protect a place, as well as the energies which are contributed by all who visit there.

To understand the nature of the spirit of a place, one must be able to conceive of a spirit which is more than a perceived personification, but a whole made up of component spirits who may be spirits of different elements of the place, such as the spirits of specific rocks and trees. Even so, this gestalt spirit may then appear or be perceived as a personification of the spirit of the place to human visitors who sometimes need this simplified perception in order to commune with the spirit.

For example, Stonehenge is a place where many tourists visit to sense the awe and wonder of an ancient magical place. The spirit of Stonehenge has inspired many archaeologists, nature worshippers, and all sorts of people to take an interest in the history and meaning of the place. The spirit of Stonehenge is made up of the spirits of the various stones involved as well as the spirit of the land itself, the wind spirits who incessantly whistle through the stones, and so on down to the individual grass fairies which cover the area.

Over the years, the spirit of Stonehenge has been altered to accommodate the energies put into it by all of the curiosity seekers to an extent that by day at least, it hardly resembles the spirit which once attracted so much attention in the first place. Yet there are those who have been there at night who sense an altered spirit of another kind, a menacing, protective spirit which would shield the original spirit of the place from the energies of so many intruders.

Another well known magical place, Brimham Rocks in Yorkshire, has a very different spirit despite the number of tourists who visit there. There are no ropes to keep visitors off the rocks at Brimham Rocks, which in and of itself changes

The author and a triple spiral design at Glastonbury Tor, Somerset

the feeling of the place from the impressions one gets at Stonehenge where the man-made barriers and guards affect the resident spirit with a feeling of restriction.

Brimham Rocks has an open, friendly feeling to it. It is often covered with tourists, yet the spirit of the place remains strong enough that it is the visitors who are altered by their contact rather than the place spirit. That isn't to say that the visitors don't leave a part of themselves behind as visitors do in all places, but that the spirit inspires a more relaxed and Earth-friendly feeling from these human visitors rather than absorbing the push-and-shove mentality that can take over in overcrowded tourist attractions. Oddly, a similar relaxed feeling is perceived at the Great Serpent Mound in Ohio despite the ropes which are meant to prevent tourists from wearing down this Red-Indian made serpent-shaped earthwork.

Magical places are not the only places which have resident spirits. As I mentioned in an earlier chapter, many nature religions believe that every place or object, natural or human made, is presided over by spirits in some form or another. I tend to agree with this belief. Other belief systems restrict this to natural places, ignoring the significance of such things as house spirits. Whatever any one individual believes, evidence can be found for some form of spirit activity nearly anywhere. This is particularly true for people who are very sensitive to subtle energies.

Places in which one will find Earth spirits include the obvious places, such as forests, deserts, mountains, etc., as well as less obvious places such as your kitchen, home garden and perhaps even your office or workplace. The sorts of spirits that one will encounter in these places vary accordingly, as one would expect, and even in ways that one might not expect. Ancient sites are easily associated with resident spirits. Graveyards or burial mounds are historically associated with

The author at Wistman's Wood, Devon

anything from a general 'feeling' about the place to strong beliefs in sacred spirits which guard the area. Visitors to many places of worship have noticed a calm feeling about these places, whether it is an indoor church or an outdoor grove or other form of Temple.

One theory which may explain spirits of some human made places and objects is explained in my book, *Understanding Chaos Magic*. I've attempted to explain bifurcation in relation to chaos science which I've also compared to Stephen Mace's explanation of virtual photons in an earlier article (*Defining Chaos, Mezlim* volII no. 2). These explanations of scientific phenomena illustrate a less complicated natural consequence of a situation where increasing stress in specific conditions result in a change in those conditions in order to relieve that stress.

The easiest example of this is boiling water. As we know, heating water will eventually result in a full boil. The heat causes changes in the movements of the water molecules, until a rather sudden bifurcation occurs and the water begins to bubble. By the same general theory, the constant infusions of energy created by attention given to a place or object must eventually result in a change of some sort. Psychically sensitive people are very aware of this when they visit historic or sacred sites. Just as a place like Stonehenge is affected by both its ancient history and the attention of throngs of tourists who visit it today, an office computer, or a child's teddy, absorbs the spiritual energy of the attention it receives and begins to take on a spirit of its own.

The natural assumption might be that a spirit of a human-made object such as a computer or a car elemental is likely to be a thought form, as these machines are very much human inventions. This is a possibility in many cases, but not always necessarily the case. The fact is that computers, cars and other human-made objects, are made from component

The Devil's Arrows, North Yorkshire

materials which at some basic level have come from materials harvested from the earth. It may be difficult to look at a glass screen encased in plastic, containing metal and more plastic parts, and see this conglomeration of artificial inventiveness as having anything to do with anything in nature, yet at some basic level these materials have been synthesised from natural building blocks of the Earth. Add to this the artificial intelligence which is programmed into the computer's artificial brain, and you have the elements of a modern form of Earth spirit - - - almost a robot elemental.

Followers of Shamanic religions believe that the spirits of a place can be disrupted by humans extracting such things as trees or minerals from the Earth, in some cases resulting in these spirits being torn away from their natural habitats. A machine that seems to operate with a mind of its own may well be reacting to spirits of its component materials which have been displaced, and may possibly be corrected by allowing a Shaman to rattle the spirits back to their home territory.

These are a different sort of spirit than the computer spirit which is formed by human attention. Such a spirit can dominate the feeling of an office, which is also affected by the people who work or visit there, as well as any number of minor elementals that may inhabit anything in the office right down to the wood in a pencil. This would explain why people often react to an office, either positively or negatively, on first impression. Some would claim that it's down to the decorators, but if you observe your own reactions to different places of this sort, you will find that your reactions are often not in keeping with your personal opinion of the decor.

Natural places are the best for attempting to sense elemental spirits. More intense Earth spirit energies may be found at stone circles and other magical places, but any out of the way place where nature can thrive undisturbed by human

Spiral tail of the Great Serpent Mound in Ohio

interference is likely to be conducive to encounters with the spirits of the Earth.

An awareness of the nature of place spirits can be a real benefit when deciding what sort of spirit one would like to have ruling one's own special places. A place outdoors to meditate or conduct rituals can be chosen according to a natural affinity with the spirit of a place, or with a bit of work and awareness of natural laws of nature, a friendly spirit can actually be invited into a place.

While I would seriously discourage anyone from randomly trying to change the spirit of a natural place where a resident spirit is already in attendance, a particularly nasty feeling place can be vastly improved through human efforts, with the intention of cooperating with nature spirits.

For example, if you know of a place where humans have dumped rubbish and the plants have mostly died, it is worth considering that you have the power to change or free the spirit of the place by cleaning it up and planting healthy growing things. If this is followed up by caring for the planted things, a relationship between you and the place spirit, as well as the individual spirits of whatever you have planted, will naturally grow and you will have created your own special place. One must, of course, consider the location and whether there may be a problem with trespassing laws.

This can also be done at home, both inside your home and with a magical garden. The feeling that one gets when entering a building, whether it is a home, an office or a shop, reveals the sort of spirit which has become the guardian of the place. All of the little things that one collects and keeps either at home or at a work place will affect the spirit of the place, even more so if these things include live things like plants or certain kinds of stones. The spirit of a human dwelling is very much affected by the energies provided by the humans who live or work there, so if your home has an uncomfortable feeling to it, it may be worth trying to get some insights into what sort of energies you are sending out.

Magical gardens are a personal favourite form of spirit magic, partly because the spirits of such a garden literally saved my life once, but also because it is possible to form very close human/elemental relationships in such a garden. I am not defining a magical garden as a garden where specifically medicinal herbs are grown, but as one where whatever you choose to grow, magic is used in the process and building a relationship with the garden spirits is a part of the project. This can be done just as effectively in a few pots as in a large plot of land.

Actually, I think the ideal location for a magical garden is a small plot, possibly separated from a larger mundane garden by a rock border, although raising vegetables with help from the devas as they do in Findhorn may seem ideal to another person. My first magical garden was done in a few pots on a concrete patio next to a car parking area. It was far from an ideal situation, but within a short while the garden became a very magical place, separated from the 'civilisation' outside of the ricketty fence, and a very powerful place of ritual.

Every morning I would sprinkle a bit of water (whether the plants themselves actually needed watering or not) while doing incantations to invite fairies into the garden. This little ritual formed a close connection between me and the spirit of the garden, which soon became an ideal outdoor temple. The flowers grew in defiance of the carbon monoxide world just over the fence, and the magic done there worked more easily than I think it might have had it been done in an ordinary indoor temple.

The spirit of a place of the Earth is not really so different from the spirit of a specific object, such as a tree. They each 'rule' over something of the Earth in whatever way is required, and care for their domain with a vigilance that many of our kind are unable to fully understand in a modern world where so many things have become all too easy. We easily forget that we are creatures of Earth as well.

Still, beneath the distractions of artificial lifestyles and our tendency to put so much importance on material things, there is a natural longing to feel connected to something of Spirit and to know that there are more important things in life than what clothes we wear or what sort of car we drive. With the progress of technology and knowledge which has dismantled the structure of the artificial religions of the past, we seek a more personal connection to the world of spirit. This may be why so many people are beginning to take an interest in the nature spirits and to look for ways to perceive them, in order to prove to ourselves that they are really there.

5

To See Earth Spirits

As I said in the introduction to the Spirits of the Elements Series, it is the perceptors in our eyes called cones which can perceive nature spirits. To see a fairy, one must try to catch it with the corner of one's eye.

I also explained in an earlier chapter that the eye is only able to perceive the waveforms of spiritual beings on the fringe of vision. One theory says that the central part of the retina in our eyes is used so much for ordinary sight that it does not respond to the more delicate vibrations of light from fairies, whereas the rest of the retina is fresh and more suitable for such uses. There is no generally accepted scientific basis for this theory, yet in a way it seems to make sense.

Whatever the physical explanation may be, the fact is that nature spirits are most often seen fleetingly just on the edge of vision, and that is part of the reason why they are known in legend for being deceptive and shy. They are actually seen with a combination of physical peripheral vision and psychic sight, both of which can be very elusive.

Those who seek to see nature spirits must learn the knack for it, which may not be as easy as the explanation sounds. The place to begin is to attune oneself to one's natural psychic abilities. It is very likely that you will learn to 'sense' their presence long before you can intentionally see them, although a fleeting surprise glimpse would not be unusual. Whether one chooses to try to 'get in the mood' by using specific essential oils, music or whatever is a personal choice. If doing a meditation with these things will help open up your psychic abilities, then by all means do it, but remember that you are dealing with creatures of nature which are unlikely to respond to human made products, except perhaps to hide from the flame of a candle if one is insensitive enough to light one in a forest!

The first thing to do is to decide which approach you want to take.

To Seek Earth Spirits in Nature

Going out into the woods is an obvious choice, although there are other places one may seek the 'little people'. This method takes a lot of patience and dedication for the average person, although someone who is particularly prone to psychic perception may possibly meet with success on the first try. To begin with, choose a place. This must be a place which is accessible and unlikely to be disturbed by other people who could disrupt the entire process by just happening by. The occasional hiker can be ignored, but it's best to keep interruptions to a minimum. You will have to visit this place frequently, possibly in all sorts of weather, so keep this in mind when making your choice.

Go to your chosen place and just sit.....and listen. This is very important. If you have ever tried to befriend a wild animal, you will know that the natural first reaction for a wild creature is to run away from unfamiliar human invaders. Nature spirits have the same reaction, and it's much easier for them to hide. Practice some sort of silent meditation, even if it is only to sit and watch, and listen. When you decide that you've had enough, go home. I recommend eating something to ground yourself at this point as such meditations will naturally raise psychic energies. A slice of bread with jam is good for this. Return to this place as often as you can and stay for as long as you can stand to just sit there. I did say that this takes patience.

You will get to a point where the place becomes very familiar and takes on a personal feeling. You will also probably try to tell yourself that you feel this way on the first time out or soon thereafter. This is natural impatience and should be ignored. It is possible that you may go through a stage where the place seems to feel hostile and uncomfortable. It is up to you whether you want to give up and try another place, starting all over again, or whether you are prepared to brave it out. If this happens, you are being tested. The resident Earth spirits may be trying to intimidate or frighten you away, or you may simply be reacting to your own vulnerability in leaving your psychic senses open. Either way, this stage will very likely pass, unless the resident spirits really are completely unwilling to have humans invading their space. If you choose to persevere, just keep going back until the place welcomes you. You'll know what I mean when it happens.

This is the time to begin to look. You're not looking for six foot tall elves out of a Tolkien novel, you're just looking at the same objects which have been in your chosen place all along. These will include things like rocks, trees, plants, etc. You may have even come to recognise birds or animals who frequent the area. Hopefully you will have left them alone, but perhaps spoken to them softly, without moving, as they pass. By the way, if you live in a place where wild animals could include large predators or poisonous snakes, insects, etc, it is best not to go too far into the wilds to choose your place. Always be sensible.

The objects in your place will be familiar, yet there is much more to them than you have seen so far. As you look at them now, see them in another way. Try to look through and around them. Try to see the aura which you know surrounds all things. This is done by very slightly unfocusing your eyes as you look at a specific object. Then shift your gaze ever so slightly and look at it with your peripheral vision. Whatever you think you see is probably really there, but you will try to get a better look and lose it. This is almost impossible to avoid. Try again. Don't push yourself for very long, especially the first time. You will have to come back and try again.

You should have something with you to leave as a gift for the spirits. A bit of milk or a crumbled biscuit is nice, or a bit of cake. Fairies traditionally love milk, but leaving a container is not a good idea. It may be possible to leave some in something which is natural to the place, a small bowl made from a large leaf or a natural indentation in a rock works well. I personally usually opt for the bit of cake, as it is also a traditional fairy favourite and is much easier to just leave without concerning yourself with containers. You don't want to leave any objects or solid signs of yourself whenever you leave this place.

Persistence will pay off eventually with this method, whether it takes two visits or two-hundred. The important thing is to believe what you see, because you will see it better another time if you know that it's really there. Having doubts will reflect in your own aura, and the nature spirits will become shy if they sense that negativity.

Remember that there are many different kinds of nature spirits in this place, and you will probably catch glimpses of different ones either at different times, or several in succession which could make your eyes flit about and even cause dizziness. Nature spirits will sometimes do this intentionally, rather like a game. It is actually a natural survival method for them as it easily confuses the unprepared human invader. The appropriate reaction is simply to enjoy the game and smile at your own confusion. If you good naturedly concede defeat and leave your offering, you are more likely to establish the beginning of a rapport.

If, on the other hand, a single nature spirit seems to appear and disappear behind an object, it is worth staying a while. It could be that you have aroused the curiosity of a particular entity. It takes a great deal of patience to sit and wait for such a creature to decide to show itself, or perhaps to run away after all, but once you have gained the attention of a particular nature spirit, it is likely to take an interest in you on future visits.

One important thing to remember with this approach is that you must never try to chase or hunt for these wild creatures. They will come to you in their own good time...or not. If quite a long time passes and no interest is forthcoming, you might want to try establishing an affinity with the resident spirits by helping the local trees and plants to grow, but you must be very careful not to interfere with nature's own plan. Don't start ripping up plants to make way for others according to your own ideas of how the area should be. Cleaning up dead leaves and planting loose acorns will do nicely. Too little work is better than too much, which can be interpreted as interference.

To Seek Earth Spirits in the Garden

Within your own garden, there are probably many Earth spirits who are already familiar with your presence, even if you only walk by the garden rather than taking an active interest in gardening yourself. However, they are more likely to take an interest in you if you have actively taken an interest in them, and particularly if you don't mind getting your hands dirty and playing an active role in nurturing the garden.

The focal point of the author's Magical Garden

There is a definite difference between taking an interest in an established garden and starting a magical garden from nothing as described in the previous chapter. As I said earlier, the latter can be done in a small area in pots if one lives in a flat or space outside your home does not allow for a 'proper' garden.

If you live in a home with an established garden, you can begin by simply spending some time with the garden every day, even if it's only a few minutes in the case of bad weather. Personally caring for the garden and taking an interest in what grows there, naturally or because you have planted it, will build a close relationship to the garden and the nature spirits which will certainly inhabit it. If someone else actually cares for the garden, you can still build a relationship by spending time there, talking to the spirits and treating the plants with the respect that one would afford any wild creature's habitat. Also, one of the benefits of a garden is that you can place a vessel of some sort within the garden as a permanent offering bowl, although leaving milk here may well attract the attention of the cat before the fairies get a chance at it.

The method for seeing the nature spirits is much the same as in the wild. The main difference with a garden is that they will be used to your presence, and more likely to show themselves more quickly.

Growing your own magical garden from scratch is highly recommended as this allows you to choose what you want to grow and to be very familiar with the individual plants and species in the garden. This aspect is the same regardless of the size of your garden. The important thing is to be able to care for the garden on a daily basis. Above all, you must not neglect the garden to the extent that it dries up and dies. If you have the sort of lifestyle which makes caring for a planted garden difficult, it may be better to create a rock garden. Rock spirits are very Earthy creatures with a different 'feel' to them than organic fairies, but they are also very magical beings. In some ways, this sort of garden could be preferable for a serious magician looking for a way to work closely with elemental energies.

There is no reason that one cannot have a rock garden within a flower or vegetable garden, and in fact the combined effect is very attractive and better balanced than either of the two alone. A non-organic focal point within a flower garden, such as the stone circle in my own magical garden, is not only attractive and quasi-traditional, but can also transform what appears to be an ordinary garden into a very effective outdoor Temple.

Rock gardens can take many forms. Most of us have seen adverts for the traditional Japanese rock gardens, which basically consist of a tray of sand with a rock or two and a small rake for forming designs in the sand. These are reported to be very calming devices and are recently being marketed in America and the U.K. as executive toys. If this idea appeals to the reader, I strongly recommend making one's own rather than buying the commercial version, or at least choosing your own rock(s).

The choice of rocks for a rock garden of any kind is important. As I have mentioned, rocks with a high quartz content are best because of the measurable electromagnetic energy charge. I personally like to collect rocks from places I visit, particularly magical places.

I also feel that it is important to mentally ask the spirit of these places for permission before taking anything away, even a loose rock lying on the ground.

One must never, NEVER bring harm to magical stones by chipping bits away from them! This would upset the resident

Earth spirits and completely ruin the possibilities of establishing the sort of relationship with the spirit of the stone which we are seeking.

Collecting special stones from these places is a magical act in and of itself. What one does with them afterwards is open to the far reaches of imagination. A single stone can be kept either displayed or put away in the home, tuned into for a specific magical or meditative purpose, or used as the beginning of a larger display or collection.

In my own case, I have chosen to make a circle within my flower garden, decorated with artificial fairy figures. Some of the larger stones came from Dartmoor, a very magical place for Earth spirits in Devon. This circle works as the focal point in my magical garden, and is a place of very strong magical energies.

Other people arrange their stones in any number of ways, creating outdoor rock gardens or indoor arrangements which are just as effective. One person I know was given a gift which is effectively a sculpture made up of small rocks, which resembles a well known stone structure. The artistry of the piece is magnificent, but more importantly, the miniature stone circle is very much alive with magic. The spirits of the component stones have combined their energies into the circle, very much in the way of larger stone circles.

Again, to see the spirits of a stone arrangement is very much like looking for the forest or garden fairies. Rock spirits are a bit more difficult to see in general simply because they do not wander beyond their stone abodes as often or as far, as the non-organic nature of rocks doesn't require the same sort of care as does growing things. Still, with patience, sightings can happen. Even more so if one tries growing crystals, as this involves more activity for the Earth spirits involved.

To See Invited Earth Spirits

Once a place is established, or even while it is being formed, one can invite spirits into the chosen location. The spirits will be there whether we invite them or not, but by intentionally inviting them, we are welcoming them and establishing a connection which we hope to nurture with them. This can be done by simply sending friendly thoughts, by doing simple incantations or in full ritual. I will have more to say about this in the next chapter. One can also simply invite Earth spirits into the home, or into a specific room, such as the kitchen or the Temple if you are in a position to keep a permanent Temple in your home.

Once you have learned to use the described method for seeing Earth spirits, it is possible to observe them in the kitchen, playing among the spice jars or any number of places both inside the home and anywhere you choose to go outside. Next time the family pet seems to be watching something that you cannot see, you may want to try to look with your peripheral vision and see if there is something there that your pet can see easier than you can. It may only be a speck of dust, but it never hurts to consider the other possibilities.

Spontaneous Sightings

Periodically, one hears of people who happen across fairies or nature spirits in the woods without warning, or who stumble into the 'Land of Faerie' as I've explained in a previous chapter. The most accepted explanation as to how and why this can happen is that for some reason, the person is particularly open to psychic vision by nature or simply at the time for one reason or another, and they happen to be at the right place at the right time. All cases are unique, but one repeating pattern seems to be that someone who is suffering from a physical hardship, such as the example given of Mr. Spare walking in the snowstorm, is more open to the world of Spirit at the time of the hardship. People who are lost, bewildered for some reason, or suffering from severe stress are also more vulnerable psychically.

In general, one cannot deliberately seek this sort of experience with any real hope of success, although magicians like Mr. Spare have discovered methods for inducing a conducive state of mind. For most people, I recommend that if such an experience should happen, that you consider yourself very privileged and simply enjoy it. Remember that the legends say that it is dangerous to eat or drink within the faerie realm, and try to keep your mind clear as best you can.

The possibility of meeting with an experience among the Earth spirits is significantly increased by taking an interest in them, and even more so for those who practice some form of natural magic. If one has hopes of an invitation into the faery realm, the best thing one can do is to invite the fairies into one's own magical realm.

6

Earth Spirits in Natural Magic

The invocation of spirits in natural magic is very different than in ceremonial ritual magic, and is in fact far more dependent on the voluntary participation of the spirit in question.

Those who have studied books on ceremonial magic will know that the sort of spirits one calls to service in this sort of ritual are a very different sort of being than the spirits of nature. I would even go so far as to say that nature spirits cannot be invoked, but can only be invited to join a ritual.

In natural magic, the word 'ritual' can mean anything from a simple act of folk magic to a full blown circle, often held in the woods or other natural setting rather than indoors. The reason for this is that nature spirits generally live in nature's realms, with some exceptions. It would be unrealistic to expect the fairies in your garden or a wild wood to come inside to join your ritual. If you want to invite these spirits to join you, you must take the ritual to their natural setting. Besides, if you could invoke a nature spirit into your Temple by your own will, chances are that the spirit in question would not be best pleased about being forced into the situation.

If you do want to perform indoor rituals involving Earth spirits, then it is the spirits who live in your home or temple who should be invited. You may want to cultivate relationships with specific Earth entities specifically for the purpose of including them in your ritual practices and create a natural habitat for them indoors, or you may simply work with Earth spirits who naturally occur in various parts of the home. This is something which will come naturally when doing simple folk spells and daily magics.

Spells which would be appropriate for involving Earth spirits specifically would include those concerning subjects which are associated with the Earth element, such as business, money, employment, prosperity, stability and fertility. Magical practices vary widely among different people depending on cultural background and magical path, but any magical system can incorporate elements which are specifically intended to attract the attention and participation of elemental spirits.

Folk Magic

'Folk magic' is a term used to describe the daily magics that we have had handed down to us through the superstitions of our forebears as well as the newer versions which are continually taught by children to each other in school. This form of magic is common to all cultures, although the methods may vary radically from one culture to another, or even from one family in the same village to another.

We are all familiar with superstitions which require that we touch wood, step over cracks in the asphalt or avoid walking under ladders. These simple superstitions are all based in folk magic. Interestingly, it is the superstitions which involve placating the elemental spirits, such as touching wood, which have best survived in our modern technological age.

If we become more consciously aware of the magical roots to these superstitions and of the uses of folk magic in general, then we can transcend the inclination to perform these habits out of superstition alone and apply the concepts of magic to the things we do in our everyday lives. We can consciously involve Earth spirits in things like growing things, harvesting, cooking, as well as such things as stone, image, tree and knot magic.

There are many forms of these sorts of magic and many books on folk magic in print, but the basic concepts of folk magic can be applied to nearly anything we do. Involving Earth spirits in our everyday magics is a matter of understanding the nature of the spirits themselves as well as the form of magic which we choose to perform.

For example, a typical knot magic spell would involve focusing on a specific desire while tying knots in a cord, which may subsequently be buried or kept in a special place. This sort of spell would actually frighten an Earth spirit, as binding spells in general are anathema to a nature spirit's sense of freedom.

However, by understanding that this is indeed the case, we can put more thought into the construction of the spell and look for a way in which the Earth spirit can play a part willingly and without fear. In this case, the first thing to do is to consider the intent of the spell. If it is a spell for prosperity, abandon the idea of a knot spell and do a coin spell instead.

A Coin Spell

A coin spell is ideal for money and general prosperity spells, although this is a tricky area of magic and success depends largely on whether the practitioner actually believes that it will work. As in all spells, it is the subtle workings of the subconscious mind where the magic actually takes place.

Inviting an Earth spirit to help may well make the difference, as this takes the magic beyond the magician and into a realm where magic is a commonplace occurrence.

Specific spells can be found in many variations, but here is a basic one which incorporates the help of an Earth spirit; First you must establish a relationship with a specific spirit or with the spirits of a specific place. A garden temple or a specific rock spirit kept indoors are ideal. You will also need a coin (preferably shiny and silver), some herbs and a container. Camomile and pennyroyal are good herbs for this. The container can be a very small glass or earthenware jar or a small bag made of natural fabric (silk, cotton or wool).

You can also add anything else which you feel will add a personal touch, such as perhaps a small green stone, but folk magic spells are very basic in nature and are generally kept simple.

Gather these things in the place you have chosen to perform the spell. Be sure to choose a time when you will not be interrupted. Calm yourself and contemplate the purpose of the spell, or use any meditation technique you prefer which will put you into an appropriate state of mind to perform magic. Next, you will want to invite your Earth spirit to join you.

I've referred to inviting Earth spirits several times in this and previous chapters, but up to now haven't gone into much detail as to how to go about this. The method you use is largely up to your individual preferences, but the basic idea is to first put yourself into a conducive state of mind, and then to project that state of mind to the Earth spirit(s) with whom you wish to communicate.

Having reached the calm and contemplative state, the most effective manner of projecting your invitation is to do it verbally. You can simply speak to the flowers, stone, or whatever object or place you have chosen, but a more effective way of reaching magical gnosis is achieved through chanting simple rhymes. Apart from the effect that this has on the subconscious mind of the magician, the fact is that nature spirits enjoy the music of the rhyme and will naturally be attracted to the sound of a soft voice in chant. Again, you want to be sure that you have insured privacy as best you can because you may feel silly chanting fairy invitations over your garden if the neighbours happen by. Stopping in mid-chant out of embarrassment can shatter the mood for the day, although it may be possible to 'cover' by lowering your voice to a murmur until the intruder has passed.

Actually, keeping the wording of your rhyme to something which might be described as twee or silly is highly recommended as the nature spirits will respond to the feeling of fun in them, even if the intent of the ritual is very serious. You will want to begin with a verse or two which has been predetermined, and then to follow it up with more spont- aneous verses which will help to focus your intent. If you feel that you are not creative enough to make up verses on the spot, try it. If it doesn't go smoothly, practice more. You may surprise yourself. Don't put too much pressure on yourself, especially over the idea that words at the end of sentences must rhyme exactly, and you can teach yourself to allow the thoughts to flow into words and create the magic in the process.

If repeated often enough, the opening verses can become a personal mantra for you which releases the creative spirit of ritual. The first verses I ever used in a magical garden are certainly silly in the extreme, yet they are effective and easily followed by verses more specific to the task. The reader may borrow these if a starting point is needed, perhaps changing them in ways that will make them more personal to you as you go along. They go as follows;

Flower fairies dance away,
Make my garden grow today,
Let them grow so tall and strong,
And last the seasons all year long,

Let them grow and let them thrive,
Show the world that we're alive,
With fairy magic dance and play,
Let magic grow in magic's way.

I told you it was silly. These verses are specific to growing a magic garden and have in fact changed over the years in small ways, but the four line stanzas have remained constant and lend themselves well to any purpose which may follow. The exact wording really doesn't matter, except in that one must always consider the meanings of words used in magic of any kind and the possible ways in which it may go wrong if translated differently than how you meant them. In the above example, the magic is tied to the growing of flowers in a magical garden. It is very effective for longer term spells. Yet the spell would surely fail if some disaster befell the garden. Even worse, the spell might turn within itself if the garden died from neglect.

Having reached a state of calm and invited the Earth spirit(s) to participate, the coin spell is 'charged' by adding something personal to the coin and herbs, such as wrapping a few strands of your own hair (three is traditional) around the combined objects to bring them together, but still you don't want to tie knots. If you have short hair, you can use a thread which has been soaked with any of your bodily fluids or anything else which will form the personal connection. Wrapping the objects is done while chanting the middle part of the spell which should be done spontaneously. Working the exact purpose or need that requires money into the chant is most effective. You are asking the spirit(s) to help you attain this goal, so stating your reasons in the process will get a better response than just asking for wealth for no apparent reason that an Earth spirit could appreciate.

It is rather important that this part is unique to each ritual rather than predetermined like the opening. The mental process involved in creating the words spontaneously is essential to the magic. Since you will probably be working alone for this, it doesn't matter if the words come out sounding stupid.

Put the items into your container and close the spell either with an original verse, or by simply repeating the first one over again. If you are going to bury the items, you should do so during the closing chant. If you are going to put the container away somewhere, you should close it at this time, then put it where you have chosen without speaking to anyone on the way.

A Knot Spell

If you have decided that a knot spell is appropriate for your purpose after all, you will still need to be careful not to offend your spirit. Secure knots are used primarily for binding and I do not recommend them when working with elemental spirits, although there is an exception to every rule.

An appropriate purpose for a knot spell that is Earth spirit friendly would be if you wanted to incorporate something new into your life, whether it is personal change, better luck in general, stability in some aspect of your life, or anything else which would be appropriate to the Earth element. With a bit of imagination, this could still be used to promote prosperity as a trend woven into your life.

The key word there was 'woven'. You will need something to weave, plait or otherwise tie together without tying secure knots. Three strands of a vine growing in the garden (not cut!) such as ivy is wonderful for this, as long as you are extremely careful not to harm the plant. If you do not have something appropriate growing in the garden or prefer to do this somewhere else or even indoors, you can use corn husks, straw or anything natural which the Earth spirit may be able to relate to. If you make corn dollies, this skill can certainly be used here.

If you are inviting a rock spirit into this spell, you may be able to use ribbons which will decorate the the rock as long as you do not bind it. Placing the end of three ribbons under the rock and allowing the length of them to hang over a table or shelf works well.

Once you have chosen your place and medium for the spell, decide on an opening rhyme which would be appropriate for the Earth spirit which you wish to invite. As in the coin spell, there are three parts to the ritual after having reached the calm and contemplative state. In this case, you will want to actually be touching whatever it is that you plan to weave together as you chant the opening invitation, after which you will begin to plait or weave as you chant the middle part of the spell. Do not tie a secure knot when you finish, but leave your medium in a position where it will be undisturbed at least for some time as you finish the spell.

A sample opening for this sort of spell might be something like this;

Ivy spirit hear my plea
And weave some magic here with me
As I weave and as you grow
Let magic's way begin to show

Then simply carry on with verses which describe your purpose. Chants of this sort can be used while doing any form of folk magic.

Other Earth Spells

One of the oldest forms of this sort of magic is simply to bury an image or object representative of the need in a plot of virgin ground, or at the base of a standing stone or special tree. You can invite the local spirit to help this basic spell with their own magic while doing this.

You can also simply ask the spirit of a tree or stone to help with a specific purpose, again either just speaking to the object or chanting a spell. Of course, acting out the need in some way also helps, which is what is actually happening when a woman crawls through a hole in a large stone (such as Men-An-Tol in Cornwall) to promote fertility. What many people forget to do while testing the magic of these ancient sites is to ask the spirit of the stones for their desire.

Yet another simple Earth magic spell is to think of your desire and draw an image which represents it in dirt. This is best done in the wild somewhere, where the image can be left to disappear slowly through natural means. In this case, I would invite the place spirit into the spell, again using the rhyme method.

There is no limit to the ways in which Earth spirits can be incorporated into traditional or modern folk magic practices. All you need is a little bit of imagination, as well as some forethought about the nature of these spirits and how they work. If we consider the Earth spirits while planting, harvesting or cooking, perhaps adding a rhyme while stirring the pot, then they become a part of our daily lives and are there when we need them for serious magic. Inviting the spirits of vegetables and herbs to strengthen us while putting these things into the stew is an old traditional form of folk magic which many people today believe adds spiritual nutrition to what we eat.

Making Earth spirits a part of one's daily life in these small ways has a spiritually calming effect on most people. For those who actively practice magic, inviting the spirits of the Earth into the circle brings something more.

7

Earth Spirits in Ritual

The calling of spiritual 'guardians' in ritual is common to several magical systems and Pagan religions, as is the conjuring of spirits in some forms of magic. Supplication to local spirits has far reaching tradition in many cultures and is still an ordinary facet of life in cultures which range from the Orient and South Pacific, to parts of Europe and across the American continent among the native peoples.

One may ask, what is the nature of these spirits and do they relate to the elemental spirits which are the subject of this book? Also, what purpose may be served by inviting nature spirits into a formal ritual?

There are different possible types of spirits involved in answering these questions. As was explained in an earlier chapter, the majority of spirits conjured during a ritual performed indoors are likely to be thought form elementals created by the magician for a specific purpose. The element attributed to that spirit is determined by the purpose and nature of the spirit as intended by the magician.

There are exceptions to this in that house spirits can become participants in ritual, either on their own initiative or by invitation. Those who call quarters in indoor rituals can create their own quarter guardian spirits, either by

deliberately spawning thought form spirits for the purpose or by inviting house spirits to perform this function.

The extent to which one can invite nature spirits into established ritual practices varies according to the flexibility of one's chosen magical path. The choice of magical path is an individual and personal decision, and I will not promote any one path over another in this series, but instead will try to suggest ways in which one may incorporate nature spirits into the spectrum of magical practices.

Calling Quarters
Not all magical systems require calling quarters, but most have some form of opening which involves forming a circle or banishing a space for the ritual. Some systems have predetermined wording for the opening, which makes it difficult to incorporate additional material or to make subtle changes in the wording in order to accommodate an elemental invitation, particularly when doing group work.

Other systems are completely flexible and can even be specifically geared toward inviting elemental spirits to join in the ritual. If the reader is working with such a flexible system, there are choices to be made as to exactly how the opening should be performed.

If, on the other hand, one is working with an established formula, it is still possible (with the agreement of all in the group) to introduce some form of connection to elemental spirits to the ritual without having to deviate from accepted practices.

In cases where the ritual is very much an established script, this may be a matter of including an Earth elemental among the magical equipment either by introducing a crystal or other stone to the Altar accoutrements with a suitable attendant spirit, or by inviting an Earth spirit into an existing piece of equipment which already represents the Earth element.

Another possibility is to create temple spirits, if the ritual is always performed in an established temple location. These would be thought form elementals in most cases, although 'house spirits' may be persuaded to perform this function, particularly if your temple is a living room, periodically converted for ritual occasions.

To do this, the item connected with the spirit would be kept in the appropriate quarter of the room which is North for most systems, although some old Hereditary systems place Earth in the South (more on this later). Decorative items in the colours green and brown or representing Earth in some way would be appropriate near this location.

The method for inviting the specific Earth spirit to occupy this position would vary according to the magical system being used. In some of the more strict ceremonial systems, there is no existing ritual for this purpose and it would be up to the members of the temple to decide whether they were willing to create their own ritual. If this is not an option, then there is still the possibility that the spirit, having had its element placed in the appropriate position in the temple, would gradually respond to the magical group's standard invocations and simply become a part of the group spirit.

Wiccans and other groups who specifically invoke elemental guardians will find it easier to work an invitation into an otherwise normal circle casting. Having positioned the crystal, stone, or whatever is representing Earth either on the Altar or in the appropriate quarter, an invitation can be made to the chosen spirit to become the guardian of its direction either as a part of the opening or within the body of the ritual.

Some covens still follow a specific opening formula, such as *"Hail to the guardians of the North,"* etc. In this case, there are two ways in which the elemental may be included, depending on the wishes of the group or the High Priestess, in turn depending on the authority structure of the group. One method is simply to add a bit onto the existing formula such as; *"...and we invite (name of spirit), spirit of the crystal of Earth, to be Guardian of the North in this and all our celebrations of the Goddess, so mote it be."*

Another method is to have an elemental dedication ritual which would include dedications and invitations for elementals for all of the directions. Wording is an individual matter and it must be remembered that elemental spirits respond best to spontaneity, but for the sake of including an example I offer the following;

The group opens as usual, then proceeds with the body of the ritual by stating the purpose for the day's work.

"We have come here today to invite the spirits of Earth, Air, Fire and Water to become a part of our circle, today and always, so long as this company shall gather in the name of the goddess (or Lord and Lady, or whatever)*"*.

This statement can be elaborated on extensively, or kept simple as is. Next, the Priestess, Priest, or whomever was chosen to perform the function steps to the North (or South) position and actually lays hands on the stone or other object which represents the Earth. In small groups, all may want to physically touch the object if physically possible. All try to attune to the spirit, as the chosen speaker extends the invitation. Note: It is best if the speaker, and as many people involved as possible, have already established a relationship of some sort with the chosen spirit.

The invitation begins by speaking the name given to the spirit, or with *"Spirit of the Earth,"* then continues: *"We invite you to join our rites and our circle, to be as one with us, and to be forever our guardian of the North* (or South). *In return, we ask that you help us to be at one with the things of the Earth, to form our magic on the solidity of the Earth element and all that it represents, and to lend us your magic in matters of the material world, if such is your judgement. Let it be so".* (or *"so mote it be"*).

The speaker, or the next person if different people have been chosen for each direction, would then proceed to the next element with an appropriate invitation and so on until all four directions have been covered, at which time the ritual closes according to the habits and traditions of the group. Eclectic groups and solo practitioners could certainly make use of the above formula, although again I stress that an element of individual creativity is far more important than reciting a pre-established ritual by rote. House spirits are far more 'tame' than elemental spirits in the wild, but even a thought form elemental has a will of its own and may not choose to participate in a group that is too dry and lacking in the sense of fun which appeals to such spirits, even the relatively calm Earth spirits.

Once a spirit guardian is established in this way, it can also be included in outdoor rituals by placing its stone or other object in the appropriate direction in any space chosen. On the other hand, you may prefer to invoke wild spirits when out of doors.

Spells in the Woods
A ritual performed in the woods, or any outdoor place for that matter, can easily incorporate the participation of resident spirits, if the spirits are willing! Consideration must be given in any outdoor setting to the fact that you are essentially a

visitor to the place, even if you have a regular place to perform your rituals, and one must remember that the resident spirits are likely to have an opinion on the matter of your presence. You cannot swan into their territory and expect them to welcome you and join your ritual without question, any more than you could barge into a stranger's house and invite them to join you for dinner at their table.

The first thing you should do when entering a space outdoors where you intend to perform a ritual is to ask the spirits of the place for permission. This can be done silently if you are on your own, or formally in a group. Your answer will come as a feeling of rightness or wrongness about the situation. If anyone in the group feels hostility, you must choose another place. This is where cultivating a relationship with a place spirit as described earlier is invaluable. An established, friendly place is a good place to start. You should still ask permission on each occasion though, just as you would normally knock on a friend's door each time you visit their home.

Having done this, there are several approaches that one might take to including resident spirits in your ritual. One is simply to invite them to join you, with no specific intent in mind. Friendly spirits can add their own power to your rituals (if they have a mind to) which can make all the difference in some spells.

Another approach is to attempt to invoke the various spirits according to their element during the opening. This can be tricky as it is all too easy to become arrogant and expect them to follow suit just because you said so, and I don't really recommend it in general.

On the other hand, if your practices include calling elemental quarters, it would be rude to leave the resident spirits out. Compromise can be difficult if your opening script is set in stone so to speak, but subtle changes which give the impression of a request rather than a demand can make the difference.

Probably the most effective way of dealing with resident spirits is to ask their assistance for the specific purpose of the ritual. If it is a celebratory ritual, this may only amount to asking them to add the qualities of their element to whatever symbolism you are attempting to portray.

However, if your purpose is a specific spell for something which falls under the rulership of the Earth element, it is possible to incite the Earth spirits to take an active role in the body of the ritual. Inviting the resident spirits to take part during the opening is highly recommended in this case as a method to attract their interest. Then, the content of the ritual should be geared to the individual purpose. This same format can be used to involve garden spirits, who would be more familiar with your presence and therefore more likely to be inclined to take part. Some example rituals, which can be adapted to any setting, are included in the appendix of this book.

Earth Spirits for a Specific Task

An Earth spirit can be raised in ritual to perform a specific task, but it can also become the focus or performer of a specific task on a continual basis. Temple spirits and protective guardians are examples of this. Nature spirits already have a task in caring for their natural habitat and are not easily tamed for tasks which are important to mere humans, yet in some cases can be very effective protective guardian spirits of a place in conjunction with our wishes.

Although using crystals for magic has come under a lot of critism in recent years due to over-commercialisation, they can actually be very effective for specific purposes for someone who is able to attune to the spirit of a specific crystal. In fact, gemstones both precious and semi-precious have a long history of magical use, often correlating colour to planetary rulership as a means for choosing the specific purpose.

Gemstones have electromagnetic charge, and this is something which experienced magicians are able to direct to some degree. It is far more effective when the magician also appreciates the nature of the spirit of the stone, and therefore seeks to work with the will of the spirit within rather than by force of his or her own will.

Quartz crystals have an especially strong electromagnetic charge, and as the most common colour is the clear stone which represents purity, it is very appropriate for clear-seeing purposes or anything which is associated with purity of motive. As I write these words, I have next to me a "star-crystal", one which has star-shaped impurities within in, which was a gift from a friend (thanks Gareth) and is used solely for inspiration while writing. The spirit of this crystal is a trusted friend who is happy to shake me out of episodes of writer's block.

I also have a necklace of clear quartz crystals which is worn only while doing tarot readings. The group spirit of the series of stones is attuned to clear-seeing, solely for divinatory purposes. I sometimes feel that it is they, rather than any other outside force, which decide for practical (Earthy) reasons to limit the amount of information that I am given during certain readings. This is a common frustration which other tarot readers will be familiar with. The cards speak the truth, but some things we are not meant to know too far in advance.

There is controversy regarding the use of crystals and other stones because the methods that commercial companies use to provide them for shops involve some pretty serious raping of the Earth. I would urge the reader to look into the origins of any stone used for magical purposes, not only for higher ecological purposes but also because a stone spirit which has been ripped out of its natural habitat by force may be unhappy about the situation and therefore less than co-operative with your wishes.

Tuning into the spirit of a specific stone with the intention of using it for a specific purpose is very similar to creating thought-form spirits. Of course, a thought-form spirit is by its very nature tuned to perform a specific task. Before I launch into this area of elemental Earth magic, I think a word about magical correspondences is in order.

8

Earth Correspondences

Associations and correspondences among various natural things are a human invention and unlikely to have much meaning to actual nature spirits. However, magicians and believers in nature religions often attach these correspondences anyway, for their own mental associations and use in ritual.

Considering that the actual Earth spirits are unlikely to take much notice of human perceptions of magical correspondences, one may reasonably ask what value there is in including this information in a book which is primarily about these elemental spirits. I do so because this is also a book about magic, fairy magic if you will, and these correspondences are a part of the associations that we learn as a part of our magic, regardless of our choice of magical path.

There is also another reason to include this information here. In the natural world, there is an inter-relatedness among all things, and knowledge of these associations of one thing to another goes far beyond a list of which herbs correlate to which planets and which stones and so on, but to inner knowledge of the reasons behind deciding why one thing relates to another or is associated with a specific energy, which is an important part of what constitutes the esoteric knowledge of a magician.

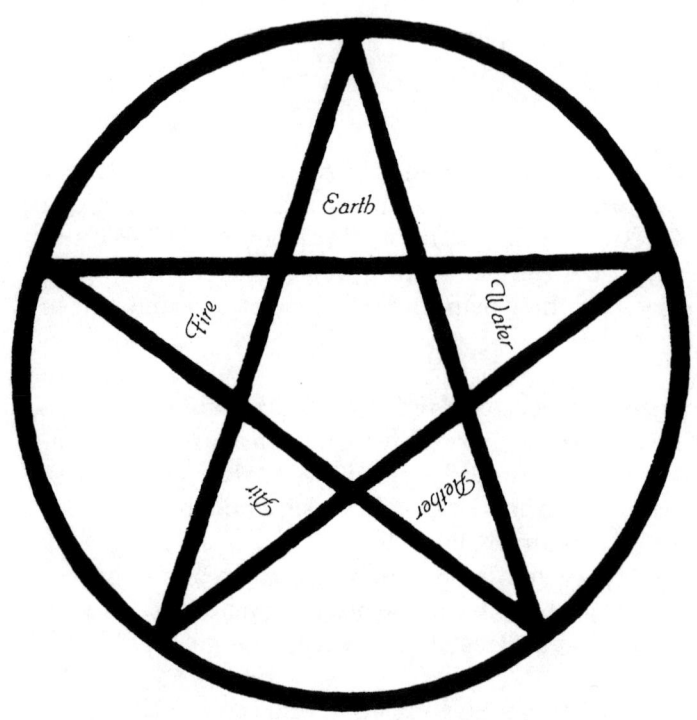

For example, if you are choosing a stone to use for a spell in which you wish to help someone with a material situation such as finding a job, you will know that you are working with the Earth element, that a green stone is appropriate for the purpose, and that this correlates with the day friday. However, friday is ruled by Venus which is more appropriate to love spells and such. Jupiter, which rules thursday, is more appropriate for your purpose. As Jupiter is associated with the colour blue, the chosen stone may be a bluish-green for this particular spell.

Those who have studied old ceremonial magic books such as the writings of A.E. Waite will know that this can all get very complicated to the point where you have to perform your ritual on a specific day at a specific phase of the Moon and conjunctions of several planets at the appointed hour, etc.

Most people today will agree with me that this degree of planning associations is unnecessary. It is the knowledge of correspondences in general which we use to get ourselves into the appropriate frame of mind for magic, and by bringing ourselves into this frame of mind, we are better able to project our intent when attempting to communicate with elemental spirits, whom we hope to include in our spells.

With this in mind, I offer the reader some basic information, charts and lists which will be familiar with many readers already, but which are sufficiently valuable to include as reminders for those who already know, and for beginning information for those who may have no experience of magic, fairy or otherwise. Each volume of the Spirits of the Elements series will include different sections of this information, in order to avoid repetition or overly long chapters of charts and lists.

I have referred several times to the compass directions associated with the elements. The majority of magical systems today agree that;

Earth   =   North
Air   =   East
Fire   =   South
Water   =   West

Some traditions have another system as follows;

Earth   =   South
Water   =   West
Air   =   North
Fire   =   East

The logic behind this is in the imagery of a man standing on the Earth, and of the universal directions of the compass points. The man stands on the Earth, above him is the Air. The fiery Sun rises in the East, and the Watery ocean is to the West (yes, there is water on all sides of Britain where this system originates, but the vast ocean is to the West while the other bodies of water have land beyond them which were within a reasonable travelling distance in the times when it was all done by ship).

The more commonly used system actually comes to us from Middle Eastern sources, as does much of our ancient knowledge of magic. The North represented Earth because that was where the mountains were, which were thought to be the home of the gods. The hottest Sun rose from the Southern hemisphere, and the hardest winds blew from the East. The ocean was still in the West, the one common point between the two systems.

The choice of which system any person uses is personal. The important point is that whichever system you use, it should hold meaning for you.

Even stronger disagreements exist when it comes to associations with magical tools. Most systems will agree that Earth is represented by a pentacle and that Water is represented by the chalice, however, disagreement exists not only between systems, but between individuals within the same systems, as to whether the sword or athame represents Fire and the wand represents Air, or that the sword represents Air and wand Fire.

This again is an individual preference and while I prefer the former system myself, I respect the right of others to choose the latter associations for themselves. Disagreement may well occur in most of the correspondences shown here, so I will simply present them in the forms familiar to me and leave it to the reader to decide whether they prefer these or different associations learned from another source.

Earth itself rules all spells and rituals concerning business, money, employment, prosperity in all its forms, stability, fertility etc.

One of the most basic systems of correspondences involves assigning metals and colours to the planets as follows;

PLANETS	METALS	COLOURS
Sun	Gold	Gold, Yellow
Moon	Silver	Silver, White
Mercury	Quicksilver	Grey, Neutral
Venus	Copper	Green
Mars	Iron	Red
Jupiter	Tin	Blue
Saturn	Lead	Black

This system was created at a time when only seven planets were known to astrologers. Gemstones have also been correlated to these seven planets as follows;

Sun	Diamond, Topaz
Moon	Pearl, Crystal, Quartz
Mercury	Opal, Agate
Venus	Emerald
Mars	Ruby, any red stone
Jupiter	Sapphire, Amethyst, Cornelian
Saturn	Onyx, Sapphire

Of course, we have discovered the outer planets since this system was devised, which renders it incomplete, but simplifies the associations of planets in astrology. The signs of the zodiac ruled by Earth are Taurus, Virgo and Capricorn. Astrological associations will be explained more fully in *Spirits of the Air*.

Much of the very concept of magical correspondences is based on the alchemical philosophy of 'First Matter'. This concept is based on the precept that the four elements; Fire, Air, Water and Earth, were first developed from First Matter. In some ways, this is similar to the 'big bang' theory which is still accepted by modern scientists.

Each of these four elements combines two of the four primary qualities which exist in all things; hot, cold, wet and dry. Fire is hot and dry, Air is hot and wet, Water is cold and wet, Earth is cold and dry. Alchemical theory accepts that everything is made of the four elements, and the differences between objects or materials are caused by the differing proportions in which the elements are combined in them. If one of the qualities of an element is altered, it turns into a different element. When Fire, which is hot and dry, loses its heat it becomes cold and dry and changes into Earth (in becoming ash). When Water, which is cold and wet, is heated it becomes hot and wet and changes into Air (in giving off vapour).

This theory was essential to alchemy because it allows the possibility of transmutation.

The ancient alchemists attributed correspondences to the basic elements for the Philosopher's Stone as follows;

Sulphur	Soul	Male	Fire
Mercury	Spirit	Male-Female	Air and Water
Salt	Body	Female	Earth

Meanwhile, Hebrew magic assigns similar attributes to the four elements in the Tetragrammaton as follows;

Yod	Fire	Hot and Dry
He	Water	Cold and wet
Vau	Air	Hot and wet
He	Earth	Cold and dry

The relationships between alchemy and the Cabalah in Hebrew magic are rather too long and complicated for the purposes of this chapter, which is intended to be a quick reference guide. To go into the subject in depth would require a separate book.

However, it is worth studying these associations whether or not the reader has any intention of looking further into the subjects involved, as the associations themselves can then become a part of one's consciousness which will affect the way in which one sees the natural transmutations in the natural world.

With that in mind, the following two pages are a basic chart of correspondences between Hebrew letters, tarot trumps, elements or zodiac signs, creatures, plants and colours.

Paths of the Cabalah

Path No.	Tarot Trumps	Element, Planet or Zodiac Sign
1 aleph	0. Fool	Air
2 beth	1. Magician	Mercury
3 gimel	2. High Priestess	Moon
4 daleth	3. Empress	Venus
5 he	4. Emperor	Aries (Mars)
6 vau	5. Hierophant	Taurus (Venus)
7 zayin	6. Lovers	Gemini (Mercury)
8 heth	7. Chariot	Cancer (Moon)
9 teth	8. Strength	Leo (Sun)
10 yod	9. Hermit	Virgo (Mercury)
11 kaph	10. Wheel	Jupiter
12 lamed	11. Justice	Libra (Venus)
13 mem	12. Hanged Man	Water
14 nun	13. Death	Scorpio (Mars)
15 samekh	14. Temperance	Sagittarius (Jupiter)
16 ayin	15. Devil	Capricorn (Saturn)
17 pe	16. Tower	Mars
18 sade	17. Star	Aquarius (Saturn)
19 qoph	18. Moon	Pisces (Jupiter)
20 resh	19. Sun	Sun
21 shin	20. Judgement	Fire
22 tau	21. World	Saturn

Creatures	Plants	Colours
Man, Eagle	Aspen	Pale Yellow
Ape, Ibis, Swallow	Vervain, Palm	Yellow
Dog	Hazel, Almond	Blue
Dove, Sparrow, Swan	Rose, Myrtle	Emerald green
Ram, Owl	Geranium	Scarlet
Bull	Mallow	Red-Orange
Magpie	Orchid	Orange
Crab, turtle	Lotus	Amber
Lion	Sunflower	Greenish-yellow
Virgin	Snowdrop, lily	Yellowish-green
Eagle	Oak, Poplar	Violet
Elephant	Aloe	Emerald green
Snake, Scorpion	All water plants	Deep blue
Scorpion, Wolf	Cactus	Greenish blue
Centaur	Rush	Blue
Goat, Ass	Thistle	Indigo
Horse, Bear, Wolf	Absinthe, Rue	Scarlet
Man, Eagle, Peacock	Coconut	Violet
Fish, Dolphin	Opium	Crimson
Lion, Sparrowhawk	Sunflower, Heliotrope	Orange
Lion	Orange Red Poppy, Nettle	Orange-scarlet
Crocodile	Ash, Yew, Cypress	Indigo

I offer no explanation as to why these things are associated with one another, but simply present them as accepted magical theory for the reader to accept or ignore according to one's own wishes.

As to how one may find use for these associations in dealing with elemental spirits, there are several possibilities. One may wish to choose plants for a magical garden according to an association of a plant with an animal energy which one wishes to associate with one's garden temple, or perhaps make an association with a tarot trump which is of personal significance in choosing colours and other decorative items for an indoor temple. The possibilities are limited only by imagination.

These associations are particularly useful in the creation of thought-form elementals, as the details of subtle energies can be very important is this art.

9

Thought-Form Elementals

A thought-form elemental is a spirit which is created out of the imagination of a magician. There is an art to creating these artificial elementals, and the reader without experience of them should be aware that there are some serious complications involved in actually exercising any control over them.

Thought-forms are essentially extensions of the soul or emotions, of the magician who creates them. However, that does not mean that the magician automatically has control over them as one would have control over the movements of one's arms and legs. Thought-forms are creations of the mind and emotions, and who among us has complete control of our own thoughts and emotions?

One of the first questions to come to mind when discussing thought forms is, "Are they real?"

Yes. They are real. The degree of effect they actually have on any given external medium is in direct relation to the amount of energy put behind their creation and sustenance, but the fact that thought-forms can have very definite effects on the material world has been proven to many an unwary soul, sometimes with very disturbing consequences.

Thought-forms are obviously different than what might be referred to here as "natural elementals", but I include them because the similarities are significant as well. The natural elemental is spawned by the need of a natural element for "being", a thought-form is spawned by a human need for "purpose". A house spirit can be either of these, or something which falls between the two. All are real beings in that they have some form of consciousness and a purpose behind their "being".

Those who are familiar with the writings of Aleister Crowley will have heard of what Crowley calls the "Magickal Childe". This is a thought-form elemental, a being created to perform a function for a magician. Magicians have created these for centuries, calling them various names. Some were convinced that they were dealing with demons, while all along they were dealing only with the demons within themselves.

Earth Thought-Forms
I cannot repeat too many times that a thought-form can and will behave independently, sometimes much to the chagrin of its own creator. The fact that magicians in history have mistaken these elementals for demons is more than the results of religious brain-washing, it is something which is easy to believe when the creatures get out of hand, which they do all too easily. If the reader is not experienced in magic, I recommend that you abandon any thoughts of experimenting with this.

Readers of Mathers and Waite will know that these historic magicians believed that they must perform their conjurations within a protected circle, commanding the "demon" to appear within a triangle drawn on the floor, which, with the appropriate conjurations, would imprison it until the magician was ready to release it to its purpose.

The problem with conjuring an elemental in the form of a demon is that it will undoubtedly behave like one, given half a chance. This entire school of magical thought is outdated and actually unnecessarily dangerous. Once you are able to accept that your thought-form is whatever you create it to be, you are better able to create a creature which will perform in the manner which you actually had in mind.

With that thought in place, your first action should be to decide exactly what purpose you want this elemental to serve.An Earth thought-form might be required if you are performing magic for material purposes; money, health, fertility etc. As with all things relegated to the element Earth, these purposes are rather more grounded and stable than much of what might be classified under the other elements, and therefore the elementals are somewhat more 'tame' and inclined toward stability. However, one should never take this quality for granted when dealing with any elemental spirit.

Of the possibilities which might be classified as Earthy purposes, the one which is both most undependable and most potentially dangerous is money. We have all seen the old horror films which depict a magician performing a money spell for someone, usually accompanied by warnings which are summarily ignored, after which the heedless client is awarded a large sum of insurance money because a valued loved one has just mysteriously died. This is not as far-fetched as the quality of these films might imply. Always, always be very specific when performing any sort of money spell, whether or not an elemental is involved. You might want to specifically conjure an elemental to 'influence' a job application or a specific game of chance. General money spells are inclined to follow the path of least resistance with no consideration of consequences.

Healing spells are generally safe by contrast. The success of both money and healing spells depends largely on the confidence of the magician, but the only real danger involved in a healing spell is the possibility of giving too much of one's own energy or empathy to the point that the sickness or injury could rebound on the healer. This is also a consideration to remember in fertility spells, especially for women.

From this perspective, a thought-form is a good choice for healing as it dissociates the healer from the patient, even though the elemental originates from the same source as direct healing energy. Fertility spells on the other hand must be handled carefully when employing elementals of any kind because there is always a danger of the entity deciding to manifest, resulting in a genuine "possession".

Apart from these common purposes for employing thought-form Earth elementals there are other situations where an Earth elemental might be usefully engaged. I have already mentioned the creation of quarter guardians for ritual purposes, but a more mundane purpose might be for help when building something. This could apply to anything, large or small. Help from an elemental can make something as ambitious as building a house into a much easier job, free of the obstacles which often accompany this sort of project. They can also help with repairs. Creating a thought-form for this comes with the added bonus that once a thought-form has become associated with a building, it becomes a natural 'guardian'.

Smaller projects may be anything from creating ritual implements representing Earth, which would then contain the spirit of the elemental, to mundane objects that suit a personal hobby. The possibilities are endless. An experienced magician knows that a part of oneself goes into everything we do. The amount of energy put into a project determines the strength of the connection. To consciously send a part of ourselves into something we make or do by creating a thought-form is the most effective means possible to bring our magical selves into operation regarding the purpose, in the manner that primal nature brings elementals into being and makes its own natural magic, which is sometimes referred to as creative chaos.

Creating a Thought-Form Elemental

Like most magical operations, this is best done in a ritual setting as it helps to focus one's energies. A ritual should be done specifically for the purpose, and not include any other matters which could cause distractions or confusion to the entity's purpose. This purpose should be very clearly thought out before you begin.

Open the ritual as usual, then focus your entire being on the purpose for your intended thought-form. If working in a group, every member of the group should be focused on the intent. It is helpful to focus on a specific spot, such as a central spot on the floor (reminiscent of the tradition of focusing the spirit in a triangle), which the individual or group can walk around in a circle* while chanting and focusing. Some examples of rituals for creating thought-forms for specific purposes are included in the appendix, but you should adjust these examples, or create your own ritual entirely, to fit your specific purpose.

If, at any time during the ritual, you or any member of the group feels somehow 'wrong' about it, the entire operation should be aborted and the ritual space should be thoroughly banished. This is very important.

Once the entity is created, it must be released to perform its function (examples also included in appendix). This is followed by a closing and banishing as in any ritual, but in this case the banishing should include specific banishings against residual energies forming into what one might call "fractal spirits". These are small thought-forms which can form from the peripheral energy raised in ritual, particularly in group rituals, which at the core are related to the purpose you have been working toward, but are more independent in that they are often left unregarded and free to develop in an uncontrolled manner. The dangers of leaving this undone should be obvious.

Having created and released your thought-form, some thought as to its sustenance is now in order.

Sustaining a Thought-Form

Thought-forms exist on aetheric energy, normally provided by their creator. Unlike their natural counterparts, they have no purpose connected to the natural world and are completely dependent on human input. However, as in nature, these artificial entities have survival instincts. Once a thought form is created, it will generally continue to take spiritual energy from its creator until it is dissipated or reabsorbed, which is something which should be kept in mind when deciding to do this in the first place. The energy to sustain a single thought-form may well go unnoticed, but sending streams of thought-forms off to do one's bidding could sap one's energy to depletion and lead to illness. It is always prudent to have a plan in place to reabsorb the entity, and therefore one's own energy, once the purpose is accomplished.

A thought-form which is left to go its own way, forgotten or abandoned, will either dissipate through the laws of entropy or will find a source of energy to sustain itself. It may continue to absorb energy from its originator without being noticed, or, if the magician has died or somehow broken the connection between them, may attach itself to another source of energy. This is a situation which is best avoided.

If you wish to intentionally sustain your thought-form, you must effectively feed it. This is done either by replenishing its energy in repeated rituals (see appendix), or through continual contact in regard to the purpose. For example, quarter spirits or an Earth elemental which is created to help with divinations. There are other purposes which might 'feed' a thought-form on a regular basis, but these are the two most common for Earth thought-forms.

Dealing with thought-forms requires forethought and judgement. One must always keep in mind that these are not personal slaves as some old magic books may imply, but are essentially elemental spirits, much like their natural counterparts.

----

*Circling around a central point creates spiral energy, which is conducive to creation of all forms of life according to natural laws which are currently being defined by chaos scientists.

10

Divination With Earth Spirits

Divination itself is generally thought of as an Earthy activity, although the widely varied forms can involve other elements. The forms of divination which are associated with Earth materials include tarot and other card readings, runes, geomancy any form which involves reading stones or bones, crystal gazing, I ching, any other form which involves coins, phrenology, palm reading, reading entrails, and astrology.

There are, no doubt, more which I have not specifically mentioned, but the general idea is that anything which uses materials of the Earth or the physical comes under the rulership of the Earth element.

Some may question whether astrology would qualify for this element because stars and planets are in the sky, and in fact astrology is ruled by both Earth and Air. Air rules inspiration which is an important factor in astrology, but it is also ruled by Earth because it is the effects of celestial bodies on the gravitational pull of the Earth and our bodies which constitutes the science of astrology. Anything which involves the use of natural electromagnetic energy, such as receiving visions while touching standing stones, is very much a thing of the Earth.

Divination does not always involve spirits, yet quite often this outside help can make the difference between the success or failure of the operation. There are times when a simple divination, using one's own natural psychic abilities is sufficient, and other times when one can benefit from spiritual assistance.

The choice of what form of divination to use is very much a personal one. It is generally more beneficial to learn a chosen form of divination well and use it regularly than to learn a little about several simply because they have each in turn become the latest popular new age fad.

This doesn't mean that one cannot learn more than one form of divination, only that it is worthwhile to concentrate on a couple of specialities that work particularly well for you, as repetition of the form builds a link between the diviner and the form. This is particularly true in cases of things like tarot cards where a lot of meanings must be remembered, unless the reader wants to refer to a book constantly while trying to receive psychic impressions.

Divination with Earth Spirits can be a very satisfying, or a very frustrating experience. As always, these spirits are independent and can be playful, yet can also be very helpful, sometimes in ways which are difficult for us to cope with. As anyone who has studied a form of divination probably knows, divining for oneself is often difficult because it is so easy to look for what you want to hear, rather than what actually is true. The divining tools will tell the truth, but our interpretation can be easily swayed by our own wishes. It is simple human nature.

Divining with the help of elemental spirits is then doubly frustrating because it is more difficult to escape the truths we don't wish to discover, yet the reading itself is likely to be much more accurate because of this.

There are two basic ways of involving Earth spirits in what-ever form of divination one chooses. One is to persuade them to oversee the operation and offer guidance, the other is to actually induce them to become associated with the medium of divination.

Invoking Spiritual Guidance

Asking spirits to oversee and guide a divination is a very simple matter, and can apply to any form of divination. A simple meditation and request, somewhat like a prayer, is all that is required.

This is most effective if the method is repeated in very much the same way every time, or directed at the same entity or entities repeatedly, whether it is a nature spirit, a god(dess) form, or a thought-form which is specifically attuned to seeking information on the astral plane.

This, as most spirit magic, is something which must be unique to each situation. The diviner might choose to invoke the spirits of a location, or a specific spirit by name. God(dess) forms are most often invoked through prayer-like dedications, but more ritualistic wording can be used for any other form of spirit.

For example, "*I call the spirit [name] to come to me and guide this reading, that I may see truth in my visions.*" Any specific wording which feels natural to the reader and conveys the meaning required can be used, and will certainly become more and more effective with repeated use.

Spiritual Diviners

I mentioned earlier that I keep a necklace of quartz crystal with my tarot cards which is used solely during readings. It is the stones which provide the actual Earth spirits who inspire my card readings and help to maintain my objectivity, in a very similar way that my inspiration crystal with its attendant spirit specifically helps me with writing inspiration and to break through incidences of writer's block.

Whatever form of divination one chooses to practice, it is possible to either associate spirits with the medium of divination or to attune a spirit to something like a stone which is present during divinations, and therefore able to assist the operation.

To attune spirits specifically to the objects used to divine is most effectively done through simple ritual. As in all rituals, this consists of a standard opening, the body of the ritual, then a closing as preferred. The body of a ritual of this sort may be a dedication of the spirits of a natural object to the purpose, a dedication of the divining method to a deity, or the creation of a specific thought-form elemental (see appendix).

Stone Tossing

Most forms of divination can be learned through easily available books. One exception worth mentioning here as an example is 'stone tossing'. The method involves collecting specific gemstones to represent each planet, which are tossed onto a velvet cloth (preferably silk, but cotton will do) and read like an astrology chart.

The cloth is embroidered with an astrological wheel, divided into twelve sections with the symbol for each astrological sign embroidered in the appropriate order. Obviously, a working knowledge of astrology is necessary for this method, although a serious belief in astrology is actually optional as it is the symbolism represented which is used in this form of divination.

The stones which represent the planets can be rough and therefore much cheaper than jewellery quality stones, The correspondences are as follows;

Sun -	Diamond
Moon -	Moonstone
Mercury -	Opal
Venus -	Emerald
Mars -	Ruby
Jupiter -	Amethyst
Saturn -	Sapphire
Uranus -	Chrysoberyl
Neptune -	Beryl
Pluto -	Onyx

Some variation is possible as long as the chosen stones are the appropriate colours. Agate and Lapis Lazuli are particularly magical stones which might be substituted accordingly. In the case of the diamond, it is possible to get an uncut diamond for a reasonable price from a lapidary shop, and is well worth keeping to the appropriate stone if possible. If this proves completely impossible, golden stones are recommended.

The stones should be kept in a pouch made of natural fibre (again, silk velvet is preferred) and only brought out specifically for readings. The method is simply to pour the stones into your hand, or into the hand of the person for whom you are reading if you choose to make a connection between them and the stones for the reading, meditate for a few moments on a question to be answered, then carefully toss the stones onto the embroidered cloth, being careful not to scatter them beyond the embroidered circle.

The stones are then read as planets in a horoscope, paying particular attention to aspects formed between them.

Whatever form of divination one chooses to practice, Earth spirits are the most potentially helpful assistants one can invoke because of their relatively stable nature, and are certainly the most reliable for telling the truth without undue confusion. It is highly recommended that one always show them respect and consideration, and to remember that they are not servants, but are friendly helpers to be loved and nurtured, as are any elemental spirits who choose to allow themselves to become involved with humans.

11

Liuing With Earth Spirits

The cycle of death and rebirth is reflected regularly in nature. Flowers die in the Winter, only to be reborn in the Spring, natural 'disasters' clear areas of the Earth only to be followed by new growth. This death and renewal cycle is relegated to the Earth element.

The Earth spirits who participate in this natural cycle each in their own way are very much a natural part of this cycle of life, and therein lies the explanation for human interest in these beings of spirit. We, as humans, are ever drawn to the magic of nature. All of us who are drawn to magic in some form are to some degree aware of the connection between magic and nature, however material our spells may be, and of the natural laws which control our ability to perform our magic.

Mankind in general has largely forgotten the connection we have to the natural world. Our artificial constructs and involvements in such imaginary worlds such as the stock market have taken over the collective thinking of a large percentage of the world's population. We have forgotten that we too, are a part of the magic of the natural world.

When we become aware of the nature of elemental spirits, we reawaken ourselves to a part of ourselves which we no longer learn from one generation to the next as a matter of course. It is up to our generation to remember the Earth spirits, and to teach our children to respect the fairies in the garden as well as the more powerful forces in nature.

Those of us who are drawn to the world of magic owe it to ourselves to learn about the nature of spirit. It is our own spiritual nature which draws us into magic to begin with. Magic is a natural part of spirit, and in turn, spirits are a natural part of magic, and can be of great benefit in many of our magical operations.

Friendly spirits are valuable friends to have indeed, and the spirits of the Earth are the most stable and enduring of all spiritual helpers. If we behave wisely towards them and treat them with respect, we can often find that the qualities associated with Earth; health, prosperity and general good fortune, will come to us naturally.

Appendix

The sample spells which follow are examples only, and not intended as a comprehensive grimoire or book of shadows for elemental spirit spells. Spells of any kind are most effective when they are constructed for the specific purpose, even more so when dealing with spirit energies who will respond to the sincerity of a spell from the heart far more than to the reading of a script.

These spells are offered primarily as models, and as a starting point for those who are inexperienced in magic and not yet confident enough to construct their own spells, or who have learned a system which may need a fair amount of adapting to incorporate references to elemental spirits. The intention is that readers should develop and individualize their own spells, whether or not they are begun from these examples, and to follow their own hearts when working magic with the spirits of the Earth.

A Sample Ritual Opening

Opening a ritual can be done in many different ways. You may choose to set up an altar, in which case you should have all of the materials you intend to use gathered and set up according to how you want them before actually beginning the spell. However, there is a tradition in magic which states that the ritual is actually started by the gathering of these items and the shift in mind-state which accompanies that process.

The purpose behind having an opening is to accomplish a shift in consciousness which is often referred to in common usage as 'ritual mode'. The items used may include representations of the four elements, representations of deity, personal items or ritual implements. Representations of Earth can be a traditional pentacle and/or an item to represent Earth more naturally such as a special stone.

The action of the ritual should also be decided in advance, especially if more than one person is involved as group actions need to be coordinated at least to some extent. An opening of a spirit elemental ritual may follow the script of a known system, or be individualized. You may choose to call elemental quarters, or the spirits as a whole, either while walking in a circle around your ritual space or while sitting or standing in one place and directing your invocation into the ritual space as would be required with a garden temple.

If you wish to call the spirits as a whole, I recommend directing your energy to an item representing each element as you say it, whether it is something you have brought or a natural example of the element which is at hand. In the case of Earth, this may be the Earth itself. You may choose your own words or use something like this;

> *"I call the spirits of Earth, Air, Fire and Water to come to me in love and magic, to bring me balance in the stability of Earth, the inspiration of Air, the passion of Fire and the emotional power of Water, and to aid that which I wish to do here now."*

From there, you can choose to launch into the purpose of the ritual or to construct a more elaborate general opening if you feel inclined to be theatrical or simply feel that more is needed.

An Opening for an Earth Spirit Ritual

If you want to invoke or invite the spirits of just one element for a purpose appropriate to that element, you can focus your full energy on a representation of that element and adjust your wording accordingly. For example;

> *"I invite the spirits of Earth to join my ritual, and to give strength to the solid foundation of my purpose, even as the Earth beneath me is the solid base of the Temple of Earth and all things which come forth from it."*

or;

> *"I call upon the element of Earth for this ritual for* (stability/fertility/prosperity/healing) *and seek within the spirit of Earth for the solid strength to accomplish my purpose."*

Calling an Earth Quarter Guardian

If you wish to call quarters, there are several books in print with scripts for known traditions. Some of them mention elemental spirits in some form or another. A standard Wiccan opening, for example, refers to the Earth elementals as Gnomes, which I personally think is rather limiting. However, it is perfectly alright to create your own wording for this purpose or to use the example which follows;

> *"I call upon the spirits of Earth, of the trees and stones, and all things of the Earth, to witness (my/our) rites and to lend their strength and stability to our magic. Let it be so."* (or *"so mote it be"*).

A Sample Ritual Closing

As with ritual openings, closings are published in several forms or can be constructed according to your own criteria. The purpose of a closing is both to make a formal end to the ritual, after which you will want to 'ground' yourself, and to banish or release any residual energies, which is very important in any form of ritual.

The wording of a closing is often related to the wording of the opening, and it is always a good idea to include thanking any attendant spirits for whatever part they have played in your ritual. Known systems will provide their own closing scripts, but closings to rituals which are opened as the above examples will require appropriately similar wording such as;

> *"I thank the spirits of Earth for joining my ritual, and for providing strength and solid foundation to my purpose. Depart now in peace to your natural realms, until next we come together in love and magic."*

or;

> *"I now release the spirit of the element of Earth, and thank you for your assistance in this ritual for* (stability/fertility/ prosperity/healing) *Let the purpose be accomplished, and the spirit of Earth be free and at peace."*

or;

> *"I thank the spirits of Earth, of the trees and stones, and all things of the Earth, for witnessing (my/our) rites and for lending their strength and stability to our magic. Let them return now to their realms, until next (I/we) call upon them for their assistance. Let it be so."* (or *"so mote it be"*).

The Middle Bit

The body of the ritual is, of course, where your purpose is defined and charged. The first step then, is to decide what that purpose will be. It is highly recommended that in any magic, this purpose should be very specific and much thought given to the chosen wording, taking note of any alternate meanings that it might be possible to read into your words. Following are a few examples of simple spells which are related to the Earth element;

A Spell for Inviting Earth Spirits Into The Garden, Temple or Home

After opening in the chosen manner, proceed with a direct invitation such as (for the garden):

> *"Spirits of the Earth, of the plants and flowers, the trees and rocks, (add any specific items which are included in your own garden gestering to each in turn), I invite you to join my garden, to help me to care for the growing things here and to bring the balance of nature to this garden and to make of it a magical place, by the power of Earth, Air, Fire and Water, so shall it be."*

(For the Temple):

Set up the Temple in the manner you choose and decide which direction represents Earth to you. You may want to invite spirits of all four directions collectively, or to face each direction in turn and invite the appropriate spirits one at a time. Opening the ritual the first time may be a bit tricky if you want to call quarters, but have not yet made the elemental spirits a part of the Temple. You can get around this complication by making the opening part of the body of the ritual and dedication of the Temple itself. Following are two example scripts for this purpose;

> *"I call upon the spirits of the element of Earth, and invite
> them to lend their strength and powers of stability to this
> Temple and the magic which will be done within it, to
> become a part of this place, and of those who practice
> with it. Let balance prevail in all workings done here."*

Proceed with the other elements, then close with;

> *"Let the spirits of the element be as one in harmony
> within this place of magic, and this Temple be dedicated
> to living in balance with the ways of the elemental spirits
> whom I have invited to become a part of this place. Let it
> be so."*

or, facing the chosen direction for Earth;

> *"I call upon the Earth spirits of the North* (or South)*,
> and invite them to lend their strength and powers of
> stability to this Temple and the magic which will be done
> within it, to become a part of this place, and of those who
> practice within it. Let the powers of strength and
> stability be the basis of all magic done here. Let it be so."*

Then proceed with the other directions and tie them together
as in the above closing. Finish by closing as you will choose to
do in future, releasing the spirits of each element in turn.
Some variations of the above examples are included in the
chapter of this book titled *"Earth Spirits in Ritual"*.

Inviting a Spirit Into a Stone or Other Object to Represent Earth

You may choose to invite an Earth spirit to inhabit an object
to be used in ritual or into a ritual implement. Earth is
traditionally represented by a pentacle which can be made of
wood, stone or metal and decorated with symbols or left plain
with just a pentagram inscribed on a circular background.

stone or crystal works well as an Earth representation, and is very portable if spells are likely to be performed in different places rather than always occuring in a permanent Temple.

To invite an Earth elemental into an object, first you must choose the object and attune yourself to the material of which it is made. Carvings or other decorations can be done beforehand, or as part of the ritual. Choose a time and place which will not be interrupted and prepare for your ritual. Outside is recommended as you are trying to enlist the co-operation of a nature spirit, but this can be adapted to an indoor Temple, relying on the spirit already resident in the stone, crystal, or natural material of your pentacle.

Open according to your chosen method. If the object is complete, you need only perform the actual invitation at this point. Hold the object and try to feel the spirit within it. If you are trying to bring a spirit into it, issue your invitation:

> "*I call upon the element of Earth, to bring forth a spirit to inhabit this* (stone/crystal/pentacle). *Let this spirit come willingly and without reservation, to become a part of the magic of this* (stone/crystal/pentacle), *and to dedicate its existence to the purpose for which it is intended.*"

You may wish to specify what the purpose is at this point, the most common purpose being "*to bring the magic of the element of Earth to my Altar*".

You may want to dedicate stones to specific purposes separately using this same formula, but never in conjunction with dedicating a permanent Altar object. Close and banish.

If you wish to decorate the object during the ritual, this is best done while stating the purpose of the object. As it may take some time to carve or paint symbols on an object, the purpose can be made into a simple chant to repeat over and over again as you work.

One very powerful form of magic is to create a chant to state this purpose in a language that you do not normally speak, as the repetition in words that you do not consciously understand will sublimate the meaning into the most powerful part of your subconscious. Be very careful of your translations! Getting the wording slightly wrong or using a phrase which can be interpreted differently than how you intend it is very dangerous.

To Sustain an Entity

Sustaining an entity which has been dedicated to a particular purpose is done by repeated use of the object, either toward actions involved in the purpose such as bringing a prosperity stone with you to job interviews, or by recharging it through repeated rituals. An Altar object is sustained through being present at rituals. Its relative strength will be affected by the frequency of use.

It is not actually possible to release an entity from something like a stone once it has been dedicated to a specific purpose. If the purpose is accomplished and you wish to do another spell for another purpose, you will need a new stone. The stone which has been used can be released into nature, perhaps to be found by someone else someday and become a 'lucky stone', or it can be kept dormant to be used again for a similar purpose.

For example, if you 'tune' a stone to help with prosperity and obtain a new job as a result, the stone can be kept for use during pay rise appraisals or for future job seeking. However, such an object should not be left indefinitely. So long as the purpose has a positive nature, it does no harm to include these objects as Altar decorations without drawing special attention to them. Objects which may have been used for something which could be detrimental to other rituals, such as reversals or anything destructive (even destroying a bad habit!) should be grounded and banished, and in most cases released to nature where they are unlikely to be found by the unwary. This sort of magic is best left to experienced magicians.

Simple Folk Spells and Other Magic

A variety of basic folk spells for purposes attributed to the Earth element can be easily adapted to include an awareness of the elemental spirits, or to directly enlist their aid.

However, many such spells concern things such as prosperity which may not be easily understood by nature spirits, and it is important to express your wish in a way that will have meaning to creatures who do not deal in business or money matters in their world. Fertility and general good luck spells are much easier to convey, but seeking aid with more material concerns is still possible with a bit of forethought.

Following are a few suggested spells. The reader is encouraged not only to use these as written, but also to use them as models for adapting other simple spells which may be collected from other sources.

Healing

In the case of healing spells, one should always do magic in addition to seeing a doctor when the affliction is sufficient to merit it. Magic works well in conjunction with science, and is not meant to be a substitute for proper medical treatment.

*To remove a disease or heal a wound, rub the afflicted area with a cut apple or potato. Become aware of the spirit of the apple or potato while chanting, *"Take this*

*(disease/wound) to the heart of the fruit, let nature's
healing draw forth this affliction from the root."*

Dig a hole in the ground (or have one pre-dug) and bury the
apple or potato as quickly as possible. As it rots, the affliction
should heal.

*If you are ill, find a patch of ground where you can lie
comfortably either on grass or bare Earth. Lie down with
arms spread and mentally see your pain, anguish or sickness
sink into the ground beneath you.

Sense the rhythm and spirit of the Earth, pulsating in time
with your own heartbeat, and feel the Earth's natural healing
energy rise into you. You should feel better when you are
ready to get up and leave.

*To rid yourself of problems plaguing you, take a handful of
Earth and draw a sigil representing your trouble in the dirt.
Become aware of the spirit of the Earth as you do this, and
ask it to take this trouble from you. Mentally project all of
your anguish into the symbol, then toss the dirt behind you
and walk away from it. Do not turn back. Mentally thank the
Earth for its healing energy as you walk away.

*To make an Earth charm, tie up a small green square of cloth
(cotton or silk) with some fresh soil so that none can escape.
You may want to include a special stone in the dirt. Carry this
with you to help give you security and stabilty in times of
trouble.

Meditation

"Strike a large, flat stone repeatedly with a dull knife. This is
best done with the stone held in one hand. Listen for the
sounds made and the rhythm which you will produce. Tune
into the spirit of the stone, assuring it that you wish the stone

no harm, but only to make music. This should quickly put you into a trance-like state.

To Charge an Object

*Make a ring of stones, preferably constructed from stones which have particularly attracted you over a period of time and which you have collected. Place the object in the centre of the circle. Trace the circle with your dominant hand, feeling the energy which connects the stones and the collective spirit of the circle.

Chant repeatedly, "*Let this (item) be infused with the energy of the Earth, and with the magic of this circle.*" Continue by stating what the purpose of the object shall be. then close with "*So shall it be*" or "*So mote it be*", Put the object in a safe place and ground yourself.

Knot Spells

Knots spells may be used for purposes of personal change, stability in some aspect of your life, to incorportate something new into your life, better luck in general, and even to promote prosperity. Always remember when dealing with elemental spirits that you must not tie a secure knot, but must leave the end open!

The method is simple; choose a medium to tie such as ivy from your garden or in the wild, ribbons tied to a stone, etc. Construct a sentence to explain your purpose. This must take the form of a positive statement rather than something to rid yourself of, as the knots or ties will secure the intent of your statement to you. Open the ritual with a petition to the spirit of the plant or stone to help bring the quality you seek into your life, and follow this with the statement, repeated several times as you plait ribbons, branches or whatever you have chosen to use. Suggestions for the above list are;

"I call upon the spirit of this (plant/stone) to secure into my life this wish of my desire;

(personal change) "I wish to breath the fresh air, free of the need for nicotene" or "I wish to face the world with confidence and positive thinking" etc.

(stability in some aspect of your life) "Let the spirit of this stone infuse me with the stability of the Earth itself, of the solid foundations which I now feel the need for (purpose).

(to incorportate something new into your life) "Let the spirit of the (stone/ivy/etc.) help me to incorporate (new influence) into my life, to feel it become a natural part of me, that I may be at peace with this new aspect of my life."

(better luck in general) "Let the spirit of the Earth within this (item) bring the positive energy of better luck into my life, and let this new energy attract good things to me in every aspect of my life."

(to promote prosperity) "I wish for the means to (live in comfort/obtain a specific item) in the world of men where these things are obtained with symbols to represent worth. Let the necessary symbols, called currency, come into my hands without doing harm to myself or any other person or creature of nature."

In the case of prosperity spells, it is important to specify a purpose for material gain, as well as to specify that the method by which it comes will do no harm to anyone, lest you find yourself collecting insurance payments. This is an important rule of any magic.

The statement must be specific to the purpose, and always, always positive in nature. Also remember when dealing with elemental spirits that you must not tie a secure knot, but must leave the end open!

Growing and Harvesting

Growing things, whether it is flowers or fruits and vegetables, can be a very satisfying experience in and of itself. Tuning into the nature spirits while planting, harvesting and cooking makes this experience truly magical.

While planting, remember that the things you wish to grow will be attended by Earth spirits. These will come whether or not you make the special effort to invite them, but doing so will help connect you to the garden and has been known to result in better plant growth, such as in the example of the Findhorn Community.

To harvest something you have planted, either flowers to decorate your table or Altar, or something which you intend to eat, it is recommended that you mentally (if not verbally) explain your purpose to the plant before cutting it, and ask the spirit of the plant either to let no harm come to the plant if you are collecting a part of it which will later be naturally replenished, or to allow itself to yield to the natural cycle of birth and death in nature, giving the life of the plant into the cycle of the food chain.

Cooking vegetables you have grown in harmony with the Earth spirits in this way is itself an act of magic. You may wish to simply remain aware of the spirit of the plant as you prepare and consume it, allowing it to fill you spiritually as well as physically, or you may wish to chant spells during preparation to invite the spirit of the plant to feed your spirit, as it feeds your body. The words for this must come from your heart, not from a book.

Spawning an Earth Thought-form Elemental

Creating a thought-form elemental is the sort of thing that one does in an indoor Temple rather than outdoors. This is a form of magic which is recommended for experienced magicians, as thought-forms are tricky creatures which can easily get out of control. Nature spirits can be mischeivous, but thought-forms are not natural creatures and can behave chaotically if they are not given adequate direction or are left forgotten.

These Earth spirits, as I explained earlier, are actually spawned from the spirit of the magician although they resemble nature spirits in character. They are useful for specific tasks, but should usually be reabsorbed unless the task is an ongoing one such as in the case of a Temple spirit.

A thought-form might be created to help influence a job application or a game of chance. They can be used for healing the body or one's energy field, or helping with a practical task such as building work, repairs, or hobby crafts. Very experienced magicians can gain information of various sorts through employing the services of a thought-form elemental.

Many old ceremonial magic books describe ways in which one might form such a spirit, but in fact these instructions come from a time when magic was greatly influenced by Christian superstition and are well outdated. Creating a thought-form elemental is actually as simple as focusing one's own energy externally to a specific point in space. It is controlling and directing that focused energy which requires experience.

Some points of reference from the old books on magic can be useful, such as using a triangle shape in which to focus the necessary energy. To create a thought-form, prepare your Temple as usual for ritual, including a triangle either drawn on the floor or made from the same material as your pentacle.

This triangle should be inside the circle, rather than outside as some old books indicate. Position it so that you are easily able to walk around it.

Open the ritual in the way that you choose, then state your purpose as, "*I wish to create a servitor, for the purpose of* (state the specific purpose)." Walk clockwise (deosil) around the triangle, focusing all of your energy on a central point within that space. Repeat the purpose over and over again while drawing circles over the space with a consecrated wand. When you have done this for what seems like long enough (you should feel an intense consentration of power built up in the focused space), release the spirit by commanding it to go forth and do it's work, then quickly close the circle and banish the space.

This all sounds very simple, but it does take some practice. The most important thing to remember is to be very specific about the purpose.

To reabsorb a thought-form, open your circle and call the spirit back to the triangle;

> "*I call now my servitor for* (repeat the purpose exactly as originally stated), *that purpose being now accomplished, and take this spirit back into its source.*"

Step into the triangle and feel the energy rejoin with your own spirit. Close and banish, and don't forget to ground yourself well.

Earth Spirit Divinations

Divination has been mostly covered in a previous chapter of this book. Besides the divination method given in that chapter, you may wish to try one of the following;

Fill a small flat bowl seven inches in diameter with dark, rich soil. Sit in a relaxed state and gaze deeply into the soil. Mentally ask the spirit of the Earth your question, then look for symbols to arise from the Earth.

Make a small sack of yellow cotton cloth. Collect seven stones as follows; White for Peace and Tranquility; Green for Love and Money; Red for Passion and Arguements; Orange for Luck; Yellow for Wisdom and Lessons; Brown for Possessions and Gifts; Black for Negativity or Hidden Answers. Charge each of the stones in the method described using a stone circle and keep them always secure in the sack. For divination, mentally ask the stones a question, then draw one from the sack for your answer. Return it for future use.

You can attune any other materials you choose to use for divination using the stone circle method, or by doing a simple dedication through ritual. This can be a matter of inviting a spirit to become a part of those materials, or of dedicating the materials to the spirit of the Earth or to the purpose of divination. You can also attach a thought-form spirit to your materials using the above method.

A Word on "Grounding"

The word "grounding" is used in many books on magic, yet very few seem to explain what is meant by this word and even fewer explain how to do it. It seems to be assumed that any witch or magician must have learned this from the beginning of their study, as well they should. However, things which are assumed can well be missed, and as this book is about the Earth element and the spiritual energies connected with it, it seems appropriate that this subject, however basic it may be, should be mentioned.

After any form of communication with spiritual energies or any magical activity, psychic centres are left open. The magician or witch will feel a sort of 'high', which is very nice but also leaves one psychically vulnerable. It is important to ground oneself. A comfortable amount of the 'high' feeling will continue afterwards and dissipate slowly.

'Grounding' in this sense is similar to grounding electricity. The excess energy needs a place to go so that it doesn't short-circuit back on you. When you have finished with whatever magical or spiritual activity you have been practicing, direct your energy literally into the ground. The Earth naturally cleanses all natural substances. Feel the solidity of the Earth beneath your feet. Then eat something, preferably something sweet. Cakes are good, because they are not only sweet but also contain flour. Grains are very good for grounding, which makes whole grain bread second best (although you can always spread jam on it).

This will lower your energies to a tolerable level, and is in fact the reason for the tradition of sharing cakes and wine after a ritual in many magical practices. Alcohol also lowers the energies.

Traditionally, some of the cake should be crumbled onto the Earth and some of the wine poured as a libation to either your idea of deity or to the Earth spirits themselves after any ritual. So ends the ritual for the Spirits of the Earth.

Bibliography

Cavendish, Richard, *The Magical Arts*. London: Arkana Paperbacks, 1984.

Cunningham, Scott. *Earth Power*. St. Paul, MN: Llewellyn Publications, 1984.

Froud, Brian, Alan Lee. *Faeries*. New York: Bantam Books, 1978.

Grant, Kenneth. *Images and Oracles of Austin Osman Spare*. London: Frederick Muller Ltd., 1975.

Hawken, Paul. *The Magic of Findhorn*, London: Souvenier Press, 1975.

Samuel, Geoffrey, Hamish Gregor & Elisabeth Stutchbury. *Tantra and Popular Religion in Tibet*. New Delhi: Crescent Printing Works, 1994.

Spence, Lewis. *British Fairy Origins*. Wellingborough: The Aquarian Press, Ltd., 1946.

Van Gelder, Dora. *The Real World of Fairies*. Wheaten, IL: Quest, 1977.

Vinci, Lee. *Talismans, Amulets & Charms*. London & New York: Regency Press, 1977.

Waite, A.E. *The Book of Ceremonial Magic*. London: Rider & Company, 1911.

Other Recommended Reading

Aburrow, Yvonne. *The Enchanted Forest*. Berkshire: Capall Bann Publishing, 1993.

Alexander, Marc. *British Folklore, Myths and Legends*. London: George Weidenfeld & Nicolson Ltd., 1982.

Anderson, William. *Green Man*. London: HarperCollins Publishers, 1990.

Arrowsmith, Nancy. *A Field Guide to the Little People*. London: MacMillan London Ltd., 1977.

Bord, Janet & Colin. *The Secret Country*. London: Granada Publishing, 1978.

Cohglan, Ronan, *Handbook of Fairies*. Berkshire: Capall Bann Publishing 1998.

De Valera, Sinead. *Fairy Tales of Ireland*. London: Four Square Books, 1967.

Evans-Wentz, W.Y. *The Fairy Faith in Celtic Countries*. New York: Citadel Press, 1990.

Foss, Michael. *FolkTales of the British Isles*. London: GPS (Print) Ltd. 1977.

Gale, Jack. *Goddesses, Guardians & Groves-Awakening the Spirit of the Land*, Berkshire: Capall Bann Publishing, 1996.

Hadingham, Evan. *Circles and Standing Stones*. London: William Heinemann Ltd. 1976.

Haining, Peter, *The Irish Leprechaun's Kingdom*. Granda Publishing Ltd. 1981.

Heselton, Phillip. *Secret Places of the Goddess*. Berkshire: Capall Bann Publishing, 1996.

Jones, Gwyn & Thomas. *The Mabinogion*. Netherlands: Dragon's Dream B.V., 1982.

MacLellan, Gordon. *Talking to the Earth*. Berkshire: Capall Bann Publishing, 1996.

Mac Manus, D.A. *The Middle Kingdom*. London: Max Parish & Co. Ltd., 1959.

Michell, John. *Megalithomania* London: Thames & Hudson, 1982.

Pennick, Nigel. *The Oracle of Geomancy*. Berkshire: Capall Bann Publishing, 1996.

Wilson, Steve. *Robin Hood: The Spirit of the Forest*. London: Neptune Press. 1993.

Index

magical garden, 47-48, 56-59, 67-68, 92

magical, 3, 7, 11-13, 15, 27, 30, 33, 37, 39, 41, 45, 47-48, 56-59, 61, 64-65, 67-68, 73, 75-76, 81-83, 86-88, 91-92, 96, 98, 106, 110, 115, 123, 126-128

magician, 12, 32-33, 58, 66-67, 73, 81, 83, 90, 93, 95-97, 99, 124, 126-127

magics, 64-65

material, 7, 11-13, 18, 36, 49, 75, 78, 85, 93, 96, 109, 117, 119, 122, 124

Mathers, 95

meditation, 52, 66, 104, 120

Men-An-Tol, 71

mind, 7, 11-12, 14, 19, 30, 45, 52, 55, 61, 65-67, 79, 85, 90, 93, 96, 99-100

money, 64-65, 68, 87, 96, 119, 126

Mother Goddess, 17

mound, 17, 33, 36, 41, 46

mundane, 11-12, 48, 97

offering, 1, 55, 57

opening, 6, 67, 69-70, 75-77, 79-80, 105, 111-115

otherworld, 33-34, 36

Paganism, 7

Pan, 25

pentacle, 11, 87, 112, 116-117, 124

perceptors, 51

personal change, 69, 121-122

Phooka, 23

physical, 12-13, 51, 60, 101

Pixies, 22

primordial chaos, 16

prosperity, 11, 13, 64-65, 69, 87, 110, 113-114, 118-119, 121-122

quartz, 30, 58, 81, 88, 104

religion, 128

rhyme, 67, 70-71

rhythm, 120

ritual, 8, 48, 60, 63-64, 67, 69-70, 73, 75-80, 83, 85, 97-99, 105, 111-117, 121, 124-127

Shaman, 45

Skara Brae, 17

Spare, Austin Osman, 33, 60-61, 128

spell, 18, 65-66, 68-71, 80, 85, 96-97, 111, 115, 118

spontaneous, 60, 67

Spriggans, 21

stability, 64, 69, 87, 96, 112-114, 116, 121-122

standing stone, 15, 71

stone circle, 58-59, 126

Stonehenge, 15, 39, 41, 43

subconscious, 65, 67, 118

superstition, 19, 33, 65, 124

sword, 87

symbiotic, 26

system, 26, 64, 75-76, 86-88, 111-112

FREE DETAILED CATALOGUE

A detailed illustrated catalogue is available on request, SAE or International Postal Coupon appreciated. **Titles can be ordered direct from Capall Bann, post free in the UK** (cheque or PO with order) or from good bookshops and specialist outlets. Titles currently available include:

Animals, Mind Body Spirit & Folklore
Angels and Goddesses - Celtic Christianity & Paganism by Michael Howard
Arthur - The Legend Unveiled by C Johnson & E Lung
Auguries and Omens - The Magical Lore of Birds by Yvonne Aburrow
Book of the Veil The by Peter Paddon
Caer Sidhe - Celtic Astrology and Astronomy by Michael Bayley
Call of the Horned Piper by Nigel Jackson
Cats' Company by Ann Walker
Celtic Lore & Druidic Ritual by Rhiannon Ryall
Compleat Vampyre - The Vampyre Shaman: Werewolves & Witchery by Nigel Jackson
Crystal Clear - A Guide to Quartz Crystal by Jennifer Dent
Earth Dance - A Year of Pagan Rituals by Jan Brodie
Earth Harmony - Places of Power, Holiness and Healing by Nigel Pennick
Earth Magic by Margaret McArthur
Enchanted Forest - The Magical Lore of Trees by Yvonne Aburrow
Familiars - Animal Powers of Britain by Anna Franklin
Healing Homes by Jennifer Dent
Herbcraft - Shamanic & Ritual Use of Herbs by Susan Lavender & Anna Franklin
In Search of Herne the Hunter by Eric Fitch
Magical Incenses and Perfumes by Jan Brodie
Magical Lore of Cats by Marion Davies
Magical Lore of Herbs by Marion Davies
Masks of Misrule - The Horned God & His Cult in Europe by Nigel Jackson
Mysteries of the Runes by Michael Howard
Patchwork of Magic by Julia Day
Psychic Self Defence - Real Solutions by Jan Brodie
Runic Astrology by Nigel Pennick
Sacred Animals by Gordon MacLellan
Sacred Grove - The Mysteries of the Forest by Yvonne Aburrow
Sacred Geometry   by Nigel Pennick
Sacred Lore of Horses The by Marion Davies
Sacred Ring - Pagan Origins British Folk Festivals & Customs by Michael Howard
Seasonal Magic - Diary of a Village Witch by Paddy Slade
Secret Places of the Goddess by Philip Heselton
Talking to the Earth by Gordon Maclellan
Taming the Wolf - Full Moon Meditations by Steve Hounsome
The Goddess Year by Nigel Pennick & Helen Field
West Country Wicca by Rhiannon Ryall

Capall Bann is owned and run by people actively involved in many of the areas in which we publish. Our list is expanding rapidly so do contact us for details on the latest releases.

Capall Bann Publishing, Freshfields, Chieveley, Berks, RG20 8TF